Praying Partners

Florence Littauer

No one prays for me and America like Evelyn Davison. For more than thirty-five years, I have observed her passion for prayer, especially for our beloved nation. Having been the recipient of many of her prayers, I know just how powerful they are. Evelyn shares concepts and experience in *Praising and Praying Across America*. It is not a book that you simply sit down and read. It is a book that God will use if you put it into practice.

Florence Littauer, international speaker, author, and
founder of CLASSEMINARS, Inc.
Palm Springs, California

Judge Edna Staudt

My dear friend and prayer warrior, Evelyn Davison, captures the heart of all who meet her. Her sanguine personality, evident by her colorful wardrobe and infectious smile, brightens any room. She tackles the most challenging tasks with bold faith, motivating compassion, and helpful hands.

I am forever grateful for the many times she has taken my hand and led us into the throne room of Father God in Heaven and her help in calling and bringing men and women to the monthly Prayer Alliance in the courtrooms of Central America.

Judge Edna Staudt, Texas Williamson County
Precinct 2, Justice of the Peace,
Cedar Park, TX

Jim & Vicki McGee

We describe her as the energizer, who just keeps going and going. Even in her middle 80s, she has never taken her eyes off the mission Jesus has given her to promote, teach, and practice prayer for Texas and America. She encourages prayer continually for our local, state, and national leaders. Her passion and faithfulness through the years has been an encouragement to us and everyone the Lord has brought into her life. *Praising & Praying Across America* is a practical tool the Lord has given her to challenge people to pray for our country at a time we so desperately need it.

Jim and Vicki , Co-Coordinators of
Texas National Day of Prayer.
Retired Campus Crusade leaders. www.ndpaustin.org

GENE BENDER

Rarely is a community blessed with a living example of spiritual leadership that is total in sacrificial service, respected throughout all civic, political, and religious arenas and has earned access to the highest levels of government. America cannot escape the uncompromising love of "The Love Lady," Mrs. Evelyn Davison. Her work to advance prayer throughout our nation has touched many. Texas and America are changed landscapes for the better because of Mrs. Evelyn.

Gene Bender, President, CEO, GLG Media, LLC,
The Bridge 1120 KTXW Radio, Texas.

ED & ELIZABETH HORNE

Evelyn Davison—the quintessential prayer warrior. Following Evelyn either through print media or on the radio will keep your prayer life grounded and on high alert. Praying for our leaders has always been one of Evelyn's passions. The great state of Texas has definitely benefitted from her prayers. ephorne@me.com

Ed & Elizabeth Horne,
Texas NDP Board of Directors,
Austin builder and developer.

CHAPLAIN KENNETH SORRENSON

Praising & Praying Across America is a book that is greatly needed. It's timing is perfect. America and our nation face an ever increasing challenging environment. Never in history has prayer been more critical. Our military men and women desire prayer more than ever. Evelyn's commitment and long-time involvement with the nationwide prayer movement has prepared her to lay out the mission and steps of effective prayer for the nations' finest servants and soldiers.

CH(LTC) Kenneth Sorenson , U.S. Army Division Chaplain,
Florida Station.

Laurie Bartlett

The remarkable lady of love, Evelyn Davison promenades, with a blessed assurance, the love Christ wants for each of us. My time with Evelyn, whether she was my guest on the radio, teaching the principles of love through her television program, or simply holding my hand will be cherished and passed on through my lifetime. Evelyn's unwavering influence reflects pain, joy, triumph, compassion, and the promise of God's love.

Laurie Bartlett M.S. HRM, On Point TV *&* Radio Broadcasting,
lauriejbartlett@gmail.com

Betty Hawley Scott

Evelyn Davison has impacted thousands of people through her intense prayer life and Christian leadership. Not only is she a strong prayer warrior, she lives the life of a woman after God's heart. She leads the National Day of Prayer for Texas and authored *Praising & Praying Across Texas*. Now it is time for Evelyn to lead us in *Praising & Praying Across America*!

Betty Hawley Scott, M Ed.
Author of *The Time Will Come*.
bscott77@texas.net

Cathy Enderbrock

Partnering with Evelyn is like drinking at the well with Jesus and the lady in need. She brings passion, purpose, and personality to all who come her way. She has been my mentor in radio, television, and public speaking. She has helped me be a real Love Lady...wife, mother, author, and good citizen.

Cathy Enderbrock, Boise Idaho, founder of Pray Today
Contact: Cathy@letspraytoday.com

Ray Garner

Evelyn Davison's heart is hooked to the Lord Jesus and Operation Christmas Child. Evelyn serves as the Central America Prayer Coordinator for OCC and has truly been an inspiration to hundreds of Central America prayer coordinators. All year long OCC is lifted in prayer, but specifically from September 1st till the end of December.

Evelyn is always there to encourage us to pray. Pray for the children, for the Gospel presentation, and for the planting of seeds that are accomplished through a simple gift.

We are prayer warriors during this time of the year and Evelyn sees to it that we are prepared for the battle. With prayers of praise and thanksgiving, she constantly reminds us to lift each other up in prayer for the benefit of the Kingdom of God. I hope to be praying with Evelyn and her team for many years to come.

Ray Garner Jr., Central Texas Church Relations Coordinator,
Operation Christmas Child.
Chaplain for Central Texas Christian Motorcycle Club.
ray@gnsinsurance.com

DAVID SMITH

Once again, Evelyn Davison has brought together some of America's most powerful and influential prayer leaders to share the practical and active habits of living a life of prayer. You will thoroughly enjoy the opportunity to learn more about the impact of prayer on the Christian life and a nation that can trust in God.

Dr. David W. Smith, Executive Director,
Austin Baptist Association
david@austinbaptist.org

Praising & Praying
Across America

Praising & Praying Across America

Evelyn Davison

Bold Vision Books
PO Box 2011
Friendswood, Texas 77549

Copyright ã Evelyn Davison 2017

ISBN 9780997851472

Cover Design by ƙae Creative Solutions
Interior Design by ƙae Creative Solutions

Published in the United States of America.

Bold Vision Books
PO Box 2011
Friendswood, Texas 77549

Bible version copyright statements are located on page188.

DEDICATION

To the Eternal Easter One named Jesus Christ,
who gives me life and hope,
I humbly submit to Him in honor and praise.

To Van Davison, the love of my life for more than 65 years,
who brings me joy and love every day, thanks and love.

TABLE OF CONTENTS

INTRODUCTION

UPWARD & OUTWARD

America is a multi-culture society—much like a family with a big heart.

From the troubles on the streets of Florida, the floods of West Virginia, and the bunkers in the Supreme Court, people are crawling out of their prayer closets. Many are seeking God's hand of provision, protection, peace, and presence for these days of terror and destruction.

As our world turns, culture is changing and people worldwide are struggling with faith, hope, and freedom.

We are grateful for the brave revolutionaries and patriots who fought and gave their lives to protect our inalienable rights of praise and prayer. The service and sacrifice of so many have protected us, making the pursuit of happiness, faith, and freedom in America a constitutional right.

The empty cross and God's people in America have become the ultimate symbol worldwide for freedom, liberty, life, hope, and faith.

America's Statue of Liberty is much like the Cross of Christ. It was dedicated as gift of friendship to America from the people of France in 1886. For 230 years, this Love Lady of Liberty planted in the New York harbor, has been the sign of welcome. It is serves worldwide as a lighthouse and billboard showcasing America's commitment to freedom and godly values.

The day Lady Liberty was dedicated, her face was covered by the French flag. People shouted as a workman climbed the 354 steps to remove the flag and show the face of the beautiful lady known as the Statue of Liberty. She stands tall, and her crown represents the seven seas and the seven continents of the world. For every man and woman, liberty is a universal yearning, not a national symbol or statue. The land of America, birthed by God, serves as a reminder of this as a welcome sign to new life.

It is the same with the cross of Jesus Christ. In reality the cross of Jesus is a powerful reminder that Jesus came to set us free and give us new life. It serves as a beacon of God's eternal love and plan for life, and an open door to a personal relationship with Jesus—God's only son.

To those who live apart from Christ, the cross is only an item—decorative jewelry, a good luck piece, or icon. For those who have experienced its mighty transformational love and power, the cross is the light of night that pierces darkness and blesses with life and freedom.

If it were not for that place and time in history when Jesus laid down his life for all, we would have no hope. His cross marks the place of grace where God opened the door to eternal life and thrill of hope.

It is with this belief that America was founded by Pilgrims and Separatists. The Lord Jesus planted them in the new world to love, live free, work, and serve. They arrived in the new land with a strong passion for freedom and had few basic essentials: the Bible, salt, soda, seeds, and soap. Life was hard as they learned to weather the storms, hunt the forests, dig God's good earth, plant, and gather a harvest. They worked and believed God for life and blessing.

Through the years America has changed drastically. Today's America is in serious trouble in every center of life.

In 240 years, America's moral and spiritual compasses have been wavering in the winds of wandering from the Truth, and worrying about wealth and politics. What America needs is not more politicians or more promises, but true patriots and people to seek God's plan and lead His way.

Today all across the nation people are struggling in doing business with God. To be a leader that people can follow to Jesus, one must know Jesus, have an intimate relationship with Him, and seek His plans for living with godly values.

That relationship starts with learning, listening, praising, and praying. The biblical admonition for praying for leaders comes from Apostle Paul in his letter of encouragement to Timothy, his young intern. Paul knew Timothy was struggling with a culture much like we have today—people who were too busy to care or were blinded with little need for God.

What was Paul's instruction? Praise & Pray!

"The first thing I want you to do is pray. Pray every way you know how, for everyone you know. Pray especially for rulers and their governments to rule well so we can be quietly about our business of living simply, in humble contemplation. This is the way our Savior God wants us to live. He wants not only us but everyone saved, you know, everyone to get to know the truth we've learned: that there's one God and only one, and one Priest-Mediator between God and us—Jesus, who offered himself in exchange for everyone held captive by sin, to set them all free. Eventually the news is going to get out. This and this only has been my appointed work: getting this news to those who have never heard of God, and explaining how it works by simple faith and plain truth" (1 Timothy 1:2-7 The Message).

This simple instruction from Paul taught Timothy the reason prayer is important and powerful today—that we might live at peace and serve the Savior. It is time in America for all of us to grow up in God's space of grace and trust in Him.

For believers, life is not a bingo hall, football huddle or a playground. It is a battleground where great moral and spiritual issues must be defended. When we are too fearful to stand for God's Truth against evil, we become defeated, lose our hope and forfeit the future of our children. America must wake up and actively report for duty, and stop sending our children unprotected into battle alone. It is not too late for us to grow up, get active, and stop hiding out in our prayer closets.

Praising & Praying Across America is about growing-up and showing-up. The Lord is challenging each of us to grow up, get out, and go tell. It is to the public places of servant hood that we are called to stand the test and deliver the message: The Lord Jesus has a love plan for each of us, and for our beloved America.

It is time for us not only to praise and pray, report for active duty, but work the fields. Why? We are to use our voice to cry out against evil as we are call on the Lord Jesus to bless America.

Jesus is our Rope of Hope, and He has planted us for times like these. As we praise Him for His love and life, we must see His wisdom, opportunity, and strength to serve Him.

> "But God forbid that I should boast except in
> the cross of our Lord Jesus Christ...."
> (Galatians 6:14 NKJV).

There are hundreds of methods for praying and praising. Some are sound, some are not, some are absolutely wonderful. None of us are able to follow them perfectly. The 7 x 7 x 7 plan for *Praising and Praying Across America* is simple. Pray 7 minutes each day for the leaders of the 7 centers of power, and the President of America, Vice-President, Secretary of State, and Attorney General.

The plan is to pray 7 minutes, 7 days a week for 7 weeks which is 49 days of praying and seeking God's plan and purpose. At end of the 49, days start over.

As you pray, do not ask for anything. Develop your "Ask Fast." Praise and thank Him for His answers and the plans He is working. That adds up to 49 days of praying and 49 days of "fasting from asking."

"Summing it all up, friends, I'd say you'll do best by filling your minds and meditating on things true, noble, reputable, authentic, compelling, gracious—the best, not the worst; the beautiful, not the ugly; things to praise, not things to curse. Put into practice what you learned from me, what you heard and saw and realized. Do that, and God, who makes everything work together, will work you into his most excellent harmonies" (Philippians 4:8 The Message).

Let us begin! As we begin, don't blink. Think.

Evelyn W. Davison

UNIT 1

AMERICA'S FIRM FOUNDATION

CHAPTER 1

AMERICA'S BANNER OF PRAISE & PRAYER

"I said to the Lord, 'You are my God!' Listen, O Lord, to my cries
for mercy! Sovereign Lord, the strong one who rescued me, you
protected me on the day of battle. Lord, do not let evil people have
their way. Do not let their evil schemes succeed, or they will become
proud... Surely the righteous people are praising your name; the
godly will live in your presence" (Psalm 140:6-8 HCSB).

Prayer and trust in God is built on a firm foundation of faith. With
one voice and one mind, our forefathers united in prayer for God's
guidance, protection, and strength. Our founding fathers specifically
called for prayer during the America's Constitutional Convention. In
their eyes, their recently-created nation with freedom to serve God was
a blessed gift. With life being a gift from God, there was only one way
to insure protection—through praise and prayer.

For Christians, this is "Communion with God." Through
prayer and praise, we experience a powerful relationship with God.
Praise is blessing God. Prayer is listening to God. Praise and prayer is
enjoying the presence and power of God.

It is our goal that you, your family, small group, or church
would participate in praying for the godly leaders you have selected
and elected. Each day brings a greater urgency than ever for Christians
to pray effectively for leaders and the cultural centers of power. We
have a unique opportunity to unite in heart and mind as we cry out to
God. "Listen to Your servant's prayer and his petition, Lord my God."
(1 Kings 8:28 HCSB).

Praying & Praising Across America is the daily discipline of prayer
built around praising and praying for the *Freedom Seven*, and making
connections, getting directions, and bringing corrections through our
chosen leaders.

Chapter 2

Adopt a Leader

My soul, praise Yahweh, and all that is
within me,praise His holy name.
My soul, praise the LORD, and do not forget
all His benefits. He forgives all your sin;
He heals all your diseases (Psalm 103:1-3 HCSB).

The 49-day journal is to guide you as you praise and pray. It will provide a way to become actively involved in what God is doing across America. The plan is to pray seven minutes a day, seven days a week, for seven weeks. A good daily plan is to pray for God's plan, purpose, and passion for America. Identify needs and blessings for the highest officers in America and their families and your adopted leader. Do this through:

Connections: Choose a leader and get to know him or her personally. Make it possible for them to know you as you build a relationship of trust. Grow your connections in your community, city and each place of leadership.

Directions: Ask for directions as to how to help and pray for them and their staffs and family. Share with them your heart for just laws, life, freedom, faith and human dignity.

Corrections: Offer positive perspective for good legislation. Work with them to preserve freedom to gather, pray, and worship in private and public places of America. Give them help and wisdom for developing relationships with other Christian leaders and stand with them against evil.

UNIT 2

AMERICA'S PREPARATION & PROVISION

CHAPTER 3

AMERICA'S BLESSINGS & PROVISION

"For all the promises of God in Him are Yes"
(2 Corinthians 1:20 NKJV).

Our heavenly Father prepared the hearts of His chosen people to believe and trust Him. He began with Moses and renewed the preparation with King David and King Solomon.

As Jesus confirmed Truth to His disciples, one of the leading religious scholars came up to Him and challenged Him. After listening to the lively exchanges of questions from followers, the guy raised a question. Struck with how sharp Jesus' answers were, he asked, "Which is most important of all the commandments?"

Jesus responded. "First in importance is to listen. The Lord your God is one; so love the Lord God with all your passion and prayer and intelligence and energy. And here is the second new commandment: 'Love others as well as you love yourself.' There is no other commandment that ranks with these'" (Mark 12:38-39 The Message).

Just as God confirmed His promises to Solomon, the King of Israel, and the disciples, He confirms them to us today.

Life's struggles are common for every generation. God's Word is filled with promises that are conditional. Jesus says, "if *you* will, then *I* will."

Jesus stood on top of the mountain and preached a sermon series using the phrase "Blessed are they *who*...." We are the "who" of today and His Word speaks directly to us. He listens to the cries of his people with His heart. He listens to *you* with His heart.

Our Father knitted each of us together, gave us life, and gave us Jesus that we might love and live both in time and eternity with him. In doing that, He made a lot of powerful promises.

"For all the promises of God in Him are Yes" was His message to the first generation of Christians and is still powerful today (2 Corinthians 1:20 NKJV).

He is waiting to hear your heart cries. He is waiting to answer you as you commune with Him through prayer.

His phone number is active twenty-four hours a day, "Call to Me and I will answer you and show you great and mighty things, fenced in *and* hidden, which you do not know (do not distinguish and recognize, have knowledge of and understand). (Jeremiah 33:3 AMP).

Do you need His help and hope? America does. Give Him a call. Prayer is the door to Christ's throne. Praise is the key to Christ's heart.

Chapter 4

America's Call to Leadership

Humble yourselves in the presence of the Lord,
and He will exalt you (James 4:10 NASB).

God's plan for America from the beginning was to raise up godly leaders to serve with humility. There is a greater need today for men and women to come forth with the attitude of serving God and a nation that is more troubled than ever before. There are three actions a leader must take. Reign, Revive and Restore.

Reign: Across America, the call is for God to hear the cries of His people for Godly leaders. The cry is, "God, send a fresh supply of passion and purpose for serving you." God says, "...as sin reigned in death, even so grace would reign through righteousness to eternal life through Jesus Christ our Lord" (Romans 5:21b NASB).

Revival: America is blessed in many ways, and yet there is great need. God says, "If my people who are called by my name will humble themselves, and pray, and seek my face, and turn from their own way, then I will hear from heaven, and I will forgive their sin and heal their land" (2 Chronicles 7:14 HCSB). This verse is a *principle* promise. "If we will, He will." The promise is valid when we follow the principle.

Restoration: Americans who are strong in faith will seek to humble themselves and believe God for freedom, liberty, and justice. God says, "Therefore humble yourselves, under the mighty hand of God, that He may exalt you at the proper time, casting all your anxiety on Him, because He cares for you...and the God of all grace, who called you to His eternal glory in Christ, will Himself perfect, confirm, and strengthen and establish you" (1 Peter 5:5-7, 10 NASB).

PRAYER POINTS FOR GODLY LEADERS

☩ Pray for the salvation of all in America who have yet to know the love of God. John 3:16–17

☩ Pray for the church in America to be steadfast in love and faithfulness to one another. Proverbs 3:3–4

☩ Pray that God will continue to place men and woman of faith in positions of authority within our government and that they will continue to live holy lives. Proverbs 16:17–18

☩ Pray for all people in America, in every sphere of public and private life, to hear the Gospel and be saved. Romans 10:9–10

☩ Pray for the church in America to share the Gospel and disciple new believers effectively. Matthew 28:18–20

☩ Pray for elected local officials to support biblical values on all local issues in America. Proverbs 21:1–3

☩ Pray that we, personally, will live authentic and godly lives, seeking revival first in our own hearts. Romans14:17

☩ Pray for the needs of those suffering in your city: the homeless, poor, sick, and lonely. Romans 12:20

☩ Pray that Christians would be salt and light, living godly lives in home and in public. Matthew 5:13–16

☩ Pray for the safety of those serving our country in the military. Pray for encouragement and strength as they are away from their families and for a safe return home. Psalm 91

☩ Pray that Christians who serve in public and elected positions in America would be directed by the Holy Spirit. 1 Timothy 2:1–4

☩ Pray for safety from violence, evil, and pride. Ask that God will unite the church. 1 Corinthians 1:10

☩ Pray for pastors to have boldness as they proclaim the Gospel and lead congregations in America. Acts 9:28

☩ Pray for the church to be aware of areas of sin, to be cleansed where there is error, and to be established where there is good. Ephesians 4:1–3

✝ Pray for Christians to repent of sin and experience a season of revival from the Lord. Act 3:19

✝ Pray for a renewed revelation of God's Word that leads to an authentic love for God and holy living. Hebrews 4:12

✝ Pray for pastors and families in America to be strengthened. 1 Corinthians 9:16

✝ Pray for Christians to be salt and light to America through humble hearts, acts of service, and the sharing of the Gospel. John 13:34–35

✝ Pray for wisdom for individuals in leadership as they make decisions for communities and the nation. James 1:5

✝ Pray for strength for God's people to uphold justice and stand against sin in the world. Psalm 7

✝ Pray for peace and calmness in the streets and neighborhoods of America. Matthew 5:9

✝ Pray for the Lord to guide the leaders of all nations and help them bring truth and light into the world. Colossians 1:9

✝ Pray for revival in our cities, our states, our nation, and all nations. Psalm 51:10–12

✝ Call on the Name of the Lord and pray for forgiveness. Ask the Lord to revive our hearts and souls. Jeremiah 29:12–14

✝ Pray for the Lord to help us, our families, and our churches live out biblical principles in every area of life. Psalm 121

✝ Pray for the church in America to be steadfast, strong, and abounding in the work of the Lord. 1 Corinthians 15:58

UNIT 3

AMERICA PRAISE & PRAYER POWER

CHAPTER 5

POWER IN THE DELIVERY ROOM

God made a promise. His children waited and waited for Him to fulfill it. Finally, the angels of heaven brought the good news to the shepherds who were on duty in the field. Their wait was over. The Savior had arrived and there was light, love, and life.

God named him Emanuel (God with Us). He walked and talked with Peter and the apostles for three years. They heard His heart, saw His miracles and wept as the enemy and political leadership plotted against Him. They saw Him crucified for a crime He did not commit and experienced His disappearance in shock.

Their joy of being with Jesus turned to mourning and fear. In all of this, they were waiting for the next great thing. Then it happened! The body of Christ that was buried in the grave of grace was raised from the dead. They praised Him as they witnessed His return and His gifts of grace and forgiveness. Jesus told them to wait and not run away. "Do not leave Jerusalem, but wait for the gift my Father promised... the Holy Spirit" (Acts 1:4-5 NIV).

It is hard to learn to wait, to be silent and listen for His voice. It takes time, but it is not impossible. So be still and sensitize yourself to hear Him speak and see Him work. He is always available to you as He waits for you to cry out to Him.

The greatest Love Gift is His presence and power. You don't have to wait any longer to invite Him into your heart! No more waiting for His love, presence, and power gifts.

"See what great love the Father has lavished on us, that we should be called children of God! And that is what we are!" (1 John 3:1 NIV).

His love gift is free. It is called grace and it will meet every need of your life. It is a gift and it is not for barter or sale.

As you seek God's love gift of grace, invite Him in to bring His life into your life. He will take permanent residence and never leave you.

Prayer for New Life.

God knows your heart and is not gravely concerned with your words as He is with the attitude of your heart. Pray this prayer and accept His wonderful gift of the abundant life.

Lord Jesus, I am lost in a world of worry and terror. I need you.
I believe that you died on the cross for my sins.
I believe you are at the door of my heart waiting for me to invite you in
and receive you as my Lord and Savior.
Thank you for dying for me and forgiving my sins
and giving me life eternal with you.
I surrender my will and way and ask you to
take control of the throne of my life.
Make me over in your image and
give me power to be just like you.

If you have prayed this prayer, write a letter to Jesus. Mail a copy of it to Love Talk Network, P. O. Box 170069, Austin, TX 78717-0069, and we will mail you a copy of the Bible and some helps for living His life of love.

Chapter 6

Power of Praise

God is love and He is great and mighty. He is worthy of continual praise and adoration. He is majestic and unsearchable. The Bible names more than three hundred names for Him. These not only describe who He is, but his attributes such as: kindness, mercy, goodness, grace, unmoving, and forever.

For some it is easy to move through praise and worship in our soul. It is also easy to close our hearts from his touch. Worship and praise takes both heart and soul. As you move through the power of praise, open your heart to a higher plain and a new level of His presence in spirit and truth. (See John 4:24.)

As citizens of God's Kingdom and the United States of America, we should stand in praise, work in praise, rest in praise and wait in praise. Thank Him in advance for answered prayer. Thanksgiving increases faith by fixing our attention on Him, not problems or needs. We bring everything to God in praise and prayer to be anxious for nothing. (See Philippians 4: 6-7.)

The closing song in God's handbook of praise and hymns is a final invitation to praise God. Thirteen times the Hebrew's song book calls for praise. It gives wisdom and direction for "Where, why, how and who."

Song Book of Praise

God—You're my God!

"I can't get enough of you! I've worked up such hunger and thirst for God, traveling across dry and weary deserts. So here I am in the place of worship, eyes open, drinking in your strength and glory. In your generous love I am really living at last! My lips brim praises like fountains. I bless you every time I take a breath; my arms wave like banners of praise to you" (Psalm 63:1, 3-4 The Message). (This Scripture is King David's praise song.)

GOD IS KING

"Robed and ruling, GOD is robed and surging with strength. And yes, the world is firm, immovable, Your throne ever firm—you're Eternal! Mighty GOD rules from High Heaven. What you say goes—it always has. 'Beauty' and 'Holy' mark your palace rule, GOD, to the very end of time" (Psalm 93:1-2 The Message).

JESUS, OUR ROPE OF HOPE

Our Lord is gracious and righteous; our God is full of compassion. "I love God because He listened to me, listened as I begged for mercy. He listened as intently as I laid out my case before him. Death stared me in the face; hell was hard on my heels. Up against it, I didn't know which way to turn; then I called out to God for help: 'Please, God!' I cried out. 'Save my life!' God is gracious—it is He who makes things right, our most compassionate God. God takes the side of the helpless; when I was at the end of my rope, He saved me" (Psalm 116:5 The Message).

LOVE'S CHOICE

"My choice is you, God, first and only. And now I find I'm your choice! You set me up with a house and yard. And then you made me your heir! The wise counsel GOD gives when I'm awake is confirmed by my sleeping heart. Day and night I'll stick with God; I've got a good thing going and I'm not letting go. I'm happy from the inside out, and from the outside in, I'm firmly formed. Now you've got my feet on the life path, all radiant from the shining of your face. Ever since you took my hand, I'm on the right way. The Lord loves the just and will not forsake his faithful ones. They will be protected forever" (Psalm 16:5 & Psalm 37:28 The Message).

O MY SOUL, BLESS GOD

"From head to toe, I'll bless his holy name! O my soul, bless GOD, don't forget a single blessing! He forgives your sins — every one. He heals your diseases — every one. He redeems you from hell—saves your life!

He crowns you with love and mercy — a paradise crown. He wraps you in goodness — beauty eternal. He renews your youth — you're always young in his presence." (Psalm 103:1-5 The Message).

Love's Blessing
"Thank you! Everything in me says 'Thank you!' Angels listen as I sing my thanks. I kneel in worship facing your holy temple and say it again: 'Thank you!' Thank you for your love, thank you for your faithfulness; most holy is your name, most holy is your Word. The moment I called out, you stepped in; you made my life large with strength. When they hear what you have to say, God, all earth's kings will say 'Thank you.'" (Psalm 138:1-8 The Message).

They'll Sing of What You've Done
"How great the glory of God! And here's why: God, high above, sees far below; no matter the distance, He knows everything about us. When I walk into the thick of trouble, keep me alive in the angry turmoil. With one hand strike my foes. With your other hand save me. Finish what you started in me, God. Your love is eternal—don't quit on me now" (Psalm 138:5-8 The Message). Praise is the password to His heart. "On your feet now! Applaud God" (Psalm 100:1 The Message).

Sing the Song of Praise to the Lord
"Hallelujah! Praise God in his holy house of worship, praise him under the open skies; Praise him for his acts of power, praise him for his magnificent greatness; Praise with a blast on the trumpet, praise by strumming soft strings; Praise him with castanets and dance, praise him with banjo and flute; Praise him with cymbals and a big bass drum, praise him with fiddles and mandolin. Let every living, breathing creature praise God! Hallelujah! (Psalm 150 The Message).

CHAPTER 7

POWER OF PRAYER

Jesus lived a life of praise and prayer. He often took time apart to examine His heart as He love talked with His Father.

The prayers of Jesus were real. It was His solemn, imperative, commanding, and royal honor to check in with His Father. Prayer was the secret of His power, privilege of His heritage, and the inspiration of His joy. It fueled His passion and purpose. It was the priority of His day.

As Jesus put prayer in a place of priority, we must do the same. This should be the heart cry of every Christian.

How can we be powerful men and women of prayer? There is no required formula, just start with praise for what He has done and will do.

Prayer is not talking to God, telling Him what is wrong and trying to get Him to do what we want. Instead, prayer is an important process through which we report for love duty and His Spirit moves and changes us. Prayer will not only transform whatever you are praying about, it will transform you.

Last fall while on vacation, I stumbled and fell, breaking my nose. Since I am a free bleeder and we were in a foreign country, it was a crisis. My first thought was, "Ut Oh!" followed by "Lord, what are you going to do now?" My second thought, *I trust you and thank you for your plan.*

What was His plan? Immediately a nurse appeared out of the gathering crowd and took charge as I prayed for a "Mercy Miracle." I got it! He also sent a taxi cab and a golf cart to pick me up and take me to the ship's emergency room where a wonderful doctor was waiting.

Why is prayer so powerful when the Lord already knows? It brings joy to the heart of God for us to seek His face and trust Him.

Prayer is a power package that the Enemy of Easter can't steal and is not words to tack on to our plans. Prayer is essential.

God's plan for *Praising & Praying Across America* is powerful. After you finish 49 days of praying, start over and practice an "Ask Fast." Fast from asking and practice praising.

Don't start with "Give me this, Lord," or the "Gimmy gimmy game." Better to start, "Lord Jesus I praise you that you have given your life for me." The Bible says, "Give thanks to the Lord, for He is good; his love endures forever" Psalm 107:1 NIV).

During these 98 days of praising and praying, our lives and our nation will never be the same. God will hear, answer, and heal our hearts and land as we pray like Jesus.

Prayer can fill your soul, bless your heart, and change your life. Together with praise, it can bring news of life, reconciliation, recovery, and restorations to America as God listens to the cries of his people.

Tips For Powerful Prayer.

WHERE?
Privately, locally, internationally. In the house of prayer or wherever you are.

WHY?
Because of Him, and what He desires to do to give us joy.

HOW?
With voices, instruments, our soul, and our feet as we give Him a life of loving sacrifice.

WHO?
Everyone who has breath and everything. Our breath comes from Him, and is the weakest thing we have.

Unit 4

America's Need for Prayer

Chapter 8

Love's Principles

America's founding fathers spent weeks seeking God's wisdom, and His plan for the future. They prayed! When God spoke to them individually and corporately, they put together some very powerful documents: Declaration of Independence, the Constitution, the Bill of Rights and others. They leaned on their Christian heritage and common understanding of law, government, social order and morality. These sprang from the system of moral and social values that were birthed in the Old & New Testament. Founding Fathers were not all totally committed to God... Their writings, their statements and their voting power is evidence that the majority of these leaders embraced great principles as the basis for a loving, civilized, orderly nation.

Accountability to God: Evil prospers **as** a nation forgets! What has America forgotten? God has a plan for America and we must one day give an account for our actions to Him. The Bible tells us that we are responsible for our actions and we are accountable for what we do... or don't do. America was birthed in the heart of people seeking to know him and serve him. They sought a community where there is a penalty for doing wrong and a blessing for doing what God says is right, noble and just.

Value of Human Life: The Bible teaches the importance of respect and preservation for all human life — from the womb to the tomb. He did not create the womb to be a tomb. All have "unalienable rights" — life, liberty and the pursuit of happiness. America was birthed on the strong belief of respect, protection and preservation of the born and unborn. This biblical principle is not just spiritual but the first priority in life.

Traditional Family: Our heritage is based on God's view of traditional marriage, family, and nation. God's plan is based on one man and one woman producing children within the institution of marriage. Preserving the traditional family is vital to the future of America.

Work Willingness: America's freedom to live independently of government is the willingness and desire to give a day's work for an honest day's pay. This spirit thrives on honor and respect instead of entitlements and handouts.

God Focused Education: "The fear of the Lord is the beginning of knowledge" (Proverbs 1:7 HCSB). The Founding Fathers believed and made education possible for America. Universities like Yale, Princeton, Harvard, and Dartmouth were all founded by Christian preachers or churches. The Bible was parent's text book for teaching their children. The New England Primer taught the ABCs with children to memorize: "A—In Adam's fall, we sinned all." "B—Heaven to find, the Bible mind." "C—Commit to Christ and He will care for you."

Common Responsibility: This is the belief that America is made up of decent people who live honest, caring, right lives. "Righteousness exalts a nation, and sin is a disgrace to any people" (Proverbs 14:34 HCSB). Americans have served as freedom fighters, food providers, health care givers for the world's poor and oppressed. The Statue of Liberty promises the opportunity to do that. "I will lift my lamp of light beside the golden door. " Love your neighbor as yourself."

God's Love Covenant: A covenant is a decision of two people or groups stating that they will keep a promise to fulfill an agreement between them forever. God made a covenant with Abraham. The covenant was: If Abraham would follow God, obeying His laws and commandments, God would bless Abraham with generations of children that would become greater than the stars or the sands on a seashore. This principle of the trust built the nation of Israel and declares that if a person or nation obeys God, observing the moral truths found in the Bible, they will be blessed. America has lived by this principle in belief that God blesses those who seek his face, follow his love covenant and listen to his voice.

Chapter 9

Love's Right

As we cry out for God's blessings on America, we must do more than ask for something or dump our troubles. Too often we shout wants and worries before we give him honor and praise for His blessings and what we already have.

Joy comes when we praise Him from whom all blessings flow, and bow and let our love show.

Americans pray for divine help, friends, families, and sometimes their enemies. But few offer praises to God or pray for politicians and nonbelievers, according to a new LifeWay Research survey.

"Most people pray when they need the red phone for help," said Ed Stetzer, executive director of LifeWay Research, adding that many of them may not have a prayer life "rooted in a relationship with God." An online survey, asked 1,137 Americans about the frequency and content of their prayers.

Among the findings:

Most prayers are personal —When they pray, most Americans (82 percent) typically focus on friends and family or their own problems (74 percent). A little more than half (54 percent) pray about good things happening in their life, while more than a third pray for their future prosperity (36 percent).

Most people don't pray for politicians. Only about 12 percent of Americans who pray say they pray for government officials, and few (5 percent) pray for celebrities. Among other things people have ever prayed for are parking spots (7 percent), other people to be fired (5 percent), or to avoid being caught speeding (7 percent). Sports teams have received a bit more prayer support (13 percent) while about one in five (21 percent) Americans

*who pray say they have prayed to win the lottery. Fifteen percent have prayed something bad they did won't be discovered. ©
www.LifewayResearch.com .*

It is unreal that more of us pray for a parking place than pray for the people who represent us in government and are responsible for our security and safety.

Could it be we just don't know how!

That is what *Praising & Praying Across America* is about. We need training and discipline in our prayer life.

The forty-nine days of *Praising and Praying Across America* can change lives: yours and those for whom you pray. Additionally, your daily prayer journal can be a page out of the Lord's history book as you identify a special need, special praise or special event —and you take time to praise and pray.

LOVE'S PRAYER

Lord, give me ARMS that I might raise
As I give you honor, glory and praise
Lord, give me EYES that I might *see*
The work that You can do in *me.*
Lord, give me EARS that I might *hear*
The cry of those who need me *near.*
Lord, give me LIPS that I might *speak*
Comfort and peace to all that *seek.*
Lord, give me a MIND that I might *know*
How to help those who need me *so.*
Lord, give me HANDS that I might *do*
Some large or simple thing for *You.*
Lord, give me a PRAYER I might *pray*
For Thy help and guidance every *day.*
And this one thing, plus all else *above*
Lord, fill my HEART so I can *love.*

Evelyn W. Davison
HE + me = WE

CHAPTER 10

LOVE'S LIGHT

It is easy to let our relationship with God suffer during times of stress or trial. There are many distractions to lead us down a road where God is not first in our lives. If you have a feeling that God is pursuing you, and leading you back to himself, don't let that feeling disappear, but revive your relationship with God as you work on these six steps.

LOVE TALK WITH HIM

Communication is essential to strengthening your relationship with God. When you say your prayers, close your eyes and picture Him next to you, listening sincerely to everything you are saying. Talk to Him as a child would talk to his or her parent. He is there to listen to all your questions and concerns and to provide you with guidance. Talk to Him as often as you can. He is there for you not only in times of need, but in times when simply need to talk.

OBEY HIM

Obey God's commandments. None of us are perfect. If we were, we wouldn't be here in the first place. We grow and develop through life so we may serve the Lord and be reunited with Him. The least we can do for Him is to try our best to obey His commandments. We should be kind and honest toward others and attend church faithfully. In obeying God's will, we become brighter and stronger in spirit, integrity, and mind.

STUDY THE SCRIPTURES

Scriptures are meaningful and beneficial study material and are necessary to strengthen our faith and relationship with God. It is one of the ways God speaks. Scriptures also give a glorious account of spiritual moments throughout time. The stories in the Scriptures deal with similar circumstances much like what we face today, at least in principle. Learning about others who have had their faith and patience tested can give us courage to prevail through our own times of trial. Making time to study the Scriptures each day will fully revitalize your tired soul.

Listen to Him

Though we may talk with the Lord often, we may not be opening our ears to hear His answers and guidance. When you are finished praying, don't quickly turn on the loud movie you were watching or immediately climb into bed for the night. Take time to stop, look, and listen for His answers to your prayers. Sometimes you may not be receiving an answer to your own prayers, but God may prompt you to be an answer to someone else's. Make sure you listen as much as you speak with Him. Communication goes both ways.

Show Gratitude

Show your Father in Heaven that you are grateful for all of your blessings. We receive blessings, and sometimes we are quick to ask for more before we take the time to thank Him. Praise Him with sincere gratitude. Being grateful for God's hand in your life will make you more appreciative of His constant presence and purpose. Being gracious goes hand-in-hand with expressing humility.

Be Mindful

Be mindful of God's presence in your life. Though it may seem like He is far away at time, He is not. He never leaves your side. It is easy to get busy and forget to look for God's presence. In these moments, be aware of how much He has blessed you and continues to bless you each day. Being humble and showing sincere love and respect for God can bring even the most deadened relationship with Him back to life. Cherish your relationship with the Lord Jesus. He is the Source of all joy and strength. The joy of the Lord is strength unmeasurable.

"Go and enjoy choice food and sweet drinks, and send some to those who have nothing prepared. This day is holy to our Lord. Do not grieve, for the joy of the Lord is your strength"
(Nehemiah 8:20 NIV).

Unit 5

America's Centers of Power & Control

CHAPTER 11

SEVEN CENTERS OF HOPE, FREEDOM, & POWER

MONDAY

CHURCH

"So then just as you received Christ Jesus as Lord, continue to live in Him, rooted and built up in Him, strengthened in the faith as you were taught, and overflowing with thankfulness. See to it that no one takes you captive through hollow and deceptive philosophy. which depends on human tradition and the basic principles of this world rather than on Christ" (Colossians 2:6-8 NIV).

PRAY:

✝ The church would find a new zeal and commitment to the mission and purpose of Jesus Christ (Matthew 22:37)

✝ Unity with and among churches that reveals God's love to the world (John 17:23)

✝ A return to the absolutes of God's Word (Psalm 1:1-3)

✝ Integrity - that God's people look and act differently than the world (1 Peter 2:11; 1 Corinthians 12:6)

✝ A holy fear of the Lord released in the heart of God's people (Proverbs 9:10)

TUESDAY

BUSINESS & ECONOMY

"I have filled him with the Spirit of God, with wisdom, with understanding, with knowledge and with all kinds of skills"
(Exodus 31:3-4 NIV).

PRAY:

✝ Integrity among Christian workers so that they win the right to be heard (1 Chronicles 29:17)

✝ Impartation of ideas and resources to open principled businesses, especially in areas that need an economic boost (Psalm 131:15)

✝ Christian workers to display Christ-like humility and service to the co-workers (Philippians 2:3).

✝ That leaders and business owners will plan no evil and do no evil that our nation's economy might be viable and strong. That every Christian leader in America would do business God's way.

WEDNESDAY

FIRST RESPONDERS
POLICE, FIREMEN AND MILITARY

"He appointed military officers over the people and assembled them ...and encouraged them with these words: Be strong and courageous. Do not be afraid or discouraged because of the king of Assyria and the vast army with him, for there is a greater power with us than with him. With him is only the arm of the flesh, but with us is the Lord our God to help us and to fight our battles"
(2 Chronicles 32:6-8 NIV).

PRAY:

✝ Courage and dependence on God (Psalm 91)

✝ Perseverance to endure hardship (Isaiah 43:2)

✝ Divine protection from the enemy (Romans 5:1-5)

✝ Wise leaders who inspire respect from those under their command (Romans 13:1)

✝ Confidence and vision to persist in the face of negative publicity (Psalm 18:31-29

✝ Protection and support for the families they have left behind (Romans 1:8-10)

✝ Chaplains who are divinely appointed to deliver hope and spiritual strength (Proverbs 4:11)

THURSDAY

EDUCATION

"My son, if you accept my words and store up my commands within you, turning your ear to wisdom and applying your heart to understanding—indeed, if you call out for insight and cry aloud for understanding, and if you look for it as for silver and search for it as for hidden treasure, then you will understand the fear of the LORD and find the knowledge of God. For the LORD gives wisdom; from his mouth come knowledge and understanding.
(Proverbs 2:1-6 NIV).

PRAY:

✝ A return to truth and Judeo-Christian ethics (Psalm 1:1-2)

✝ A safe atmosphere conducive to learning

✝ Excellence in educators (Exodus 18:30-21)

✝ Equal opportunities for every student o achieve their full potential (Philippians 1:9)

GOVERNMENT

"When all Israel heard the verdict the king had given, they held the king in awe, because they saw that he had wisdom from God to administer justice" (1 Kings 3:28 NIV).

PRAY:

✝ Government officials to recognize God's authority and rely on Him for wisdom (James 1:5)

✝ Our country to stand strong on the principles of our Founding Fathers (1 Corinthians 3:11)

✝ Our leaders to make wise decisions rather than succumbing to special interest groups (Luke 22:2)

✝ Righteous judges and judgments in every court (Isaiah 1:26)

✝ All upcoming elections (1 Timothy 1:1-4)

✝ Our Officials, Cabinet Members, Supreme Court Justices, State and Local Officials

SATURDAY
MEDIA

"Whatever is true, whatever is noble, whatever is right, whatever is pure, whatever is lovely, whatever is admirable—if anything is excellent or praiseworthy—think about such things" (Philippians 4:8 NIV). "May your unfailing love rest upon us, O Lord, even as we put our hope in you" (Psalm 33:22 NIV).

PRAY:

✝ The decision makers within the media to realize they can make profit by producing family-friendly projects (Proverbs 8:10-1)

✝ Christians in media to find favor and be filled with creative ideas that bring kingdom principles and life-giving messages to the public (Proverbs 2:1-15)

✝ Celebrities to be provided with repeated opportunities to hear and receive salvation (Proverbs 8:35)

✝ All media personnel would report what is true, noble, right, pure, lovely, and admirable as well as the hard news with truth and honor.

SUNDAY

FAMILY

"If a house is divided against itself, that house cannot stand" (Mark 3:25 NIV).

"Your love must be real. Hate what is evil. Hold on to what is good. Love each other like brothers and sisters. Give your brothers and sisters more honor than you want for yourselves. Do not be lazy but work hard. Serve the Lord with all your heart. Be joyful because you have hope. Be patient when trouble comes. Pray at all times. Share with God's people who need help. Bring strangers in need into your homes" (Romans 12:9-13 ICB).

PRAY:

✝ The re-establishment of relationships between parents and children (Malachi 4:5-6)

✝ A return to family values that serve the nation as a whole (Job 22:21-22)

✝ A return to the biblical mandate to train their children at home in the fear of the Lord and not leave the responsibility to others. (Proverbs 22:6)

Unit 6

Choosing Godly Leaders

CHAPTER 12

AMERICA'S CHOICES

ANN HETTINGER

America is strong because God's people are involved in being good citizens. One of the blessings and responsibilities of every American is being a good citizen who is actively involved. Involvement starts with praise and prayer. Americans cherish freedom to choose leaders who uphold the Constitution of the United States of America. To do that one must be acquainted and knowledgeable about issues and values. In that regard, we need to review the America's party platforms.

The following excerpts were taken from the 2017 Republican Party and Democratic Party National Platforms. They are abbreviated and compiled in comparison form.

The complete platforms are available at the following web-sites:

The 58 page 2016 Republican Platform:
       https://prod-static-ngop-pbl.s3.amazonaws.com/media/
       documents/DRAFT_FINAL[1]-ben_1468872234.pdf

The 51 page 2016 Democratic Platform:
       https://www.demconvention.com/wp-content/
       uploads/2016/07/Democratic-Party-Platform-7.21.16-no-
       lines.pdf

Statements about Sanctity of Life

The Republican Party Platform

"… we assert the sanctity of human life and affirm that the unborn child has a fundamental right to life which cannot be infringed." (Page 13)

"We urge all states and Congress to make it a crime to acquire, transfer, or sell fetal tissues from elective abortions for research…." (Page 13)

"We condemn the Supreme Court's activist decision in *Whole Woman's Health v. Hellerstedt* striking down commonsense Texas laws providing for basic health and safety standards in abortion clinics." (Page 14)

"We respect the states' authority and flexibility to exclude abortion providers from federal programs such as Medicaid and other healthcare and family planning programs so long as they continue to perform or refer for elective abortions or sell the body parts of aborted children." (Page 24)

"We renew our call for replacing "family planning" programs for teens with sexual risk avoidance education that sets abstinence until marriage as the responsible and respected standard of behavior…empowers teens to achieve optimal health outcomes." (Page 34)

"…the current Administration has promoted the notion of abortion as healthcare. We, however, affirm the dignity of women by protecting the sanctity of human life. Numerous studies have shown that abortion endangers the health and well-being of women, and we stand firmly against it." (Page 36)

"We call for a permanent ban on federal funding and subsidies for abortion and healthcare plans that include abortion coverage." (Page 37)

"We oppose the non-consensual withholding of care or treatment from people with disabilities, including newborns, the elderly, and inform, just as we oppose euthanasia and assisted suicide...." (Page 39)

"The Republican Party, a party of law and order, must make clear in words and action that every human life matters." (Page 39)"

THE DEMOCRAT PARTY PLATFORM

"We will abolish the death penalty...." (Page 16)

"We will fight Republican efforts to roll back the clock on women's health and reproductive rights, and stand up for Planned Parenthood." (Page 34)

"We recognize that quality, affordable comprehensive health care, evidence-based sex education, and a full range of family planning services help reduce the number of unintended pregnancies and thereby also reduce the need for abortions." (Page 37)

"... we believe that safe abortion must be part of comprehensive maternal and women's health care and included as part of America's global health programming." (Page 46)

"We will push for a societal transformation to make it clear that black lives matter and that there is no place for racism in our country." (Page 14)"

STATEMENTS ABOUT GENDER

THE REPUBLICAN PARTY PLATFORM

"Our laws and our government's regulations should recognize marriage as the union of one man and one woman and actively promote married family life as the basis of a stable and prosperous society." (Page 31)

"We ... support the original, authentic meaning of Title IX...is now being used...to impose a social and cultural revolution upon the American people by wrongly redefining sex discrimination to include sexual orientation or other categories.... Their edict to the states concerning restrooms, locker rooms, and other facilities is at once illegal, dangerous, and ignores privacy issues." (Page 35)

THE DEMOCRAT PARTY PLATFORM

"We believe in protecting civil liberties and guaranteeing civil rights and voting rights, women's rights and workers' rights, LGBT rights, and rights for people with disabilities." (Page 2)

"Democrats will always fight to end discrimination on the basis of race, ethnicity, national origin, language, religion, gender, age, sexual orientation, gender identity, or disability." (Page 18)

"After 240 years, we will finally enshrine the rights of women in the Constitution by passing the Equal Rights Amendment." (Page 18)

"We will also fight for comprehensive federal non-discrimination protections for all LGBT Americans, to guarantee equal rights in areas such as housing, employment, public accommodations, credit, jury service, education, and federal funding. We will oppose all state efforts to discriminate against LGBT individuals, including legislation that restricts the right to access public spaces." (Page 19)

"Democrats believe that LBGT rights are human rights and that American foreign policy should advance the ability of all persons to live with dignity, security, and respect, regardless of who they are or who they love." (Page 46)"

STATEMENTS ABOUT FREEDOM OF RELIGION

THE REPUBLICAN PARTY PLATFORM

"Because of the vital role of religious organizations, charities, and fraternal benevolent societies in fostering generosity and patriotism, they should not be subject to taxation and donations to them should remain deductible." (Page 2)

"Religious freedom in the Bill of Rights protects the right of the people to practice their faith in their everyday lives." (Page 11)

"Republicans believe the federal government, specifically the IRS, is constitutionally prohibited from policing or censoring speech based on religious convictions or beliefs, and therefore we urge the repeal of the Johnson Amendment." (Page 11)

"We support the right of the people to conduct their businesses in accordance with their religious beliefs and condemn public officials who have proposed boycotts against businesses that support traditional marriage." (Page 12)

"We likewise call for an end to the so-called Fairness Doctrine, and support free-market approaches to free speech unregulated by government." (Page 12)

"We support the rights of conscience of military chaplains of all faiths to practice their faith free from political interference...will protect the religious freedom of all military members, especially chaplains, and will not tolerate attempts to ban Bibles or religious symbols from military facilities." (Page 43)

"... a Republican administration will return the advocacy of religious liberty to a central place in its diplomacy, will quickly designate the systematic killing of religious and ethnic minorities a genocide, and will work with leaders of other nations to condemn and combat genocidal acts." (Page 52)

THE DEMOCRAT PARTY PLATFORM

"We support a progressive vision of religious freedom that respects pluralism and rejects the misuse of religion to discriminate. We believe in lifting up and valuing the good work of people of faith and religious organizations and finding ways to support that work where possible." (Page 19)

STATEMENTS ABOUT NATIONAL SOVEREIGNTY

THE REPUBLICAN PARTY PLATFORM

"To protect our national security interests and foster innovation and competitiveness, we must sustain our preeminence in space by launching more scientific missions, guaranteeing unfettered access, and ensuring that our space-related industries remain a source of scientific leadership and education." (Page 6)

America's Electric Grid ... is aging, vulnerable to cyber and terrorist threats, and unprepared to serve our energy needs of tomorrow. ... We support ... expedited siting processes and the thoughtful expansion of the grid ... (Page 6)

"We recommend...enactment by the full Congress...ways to secure the integrity of our currency." (Page 7)

"We therefore oppose the adoption or ratification of treaties that would weaken or encroach upon American sovereignty or that could be construed by courts to do so. We will not recognize as binding upon the United States any international agreement forged without the constitutionally required assent of two-thirds of the United States Senate." (Page 10)

"We call on Congress to begin reclaiming its constitutional powers from the bureaucratic state by requiring that major new federal regulations be approved by Congress before they can take effect...." (Page 10)

"We do not support the U.N. Convention on Women's Rights, the Convention on the Rights of the Child, the Convention on the Rights of Persons with Disabilities and the U.N. Arms Trade Treaty as well as various declarations from the U.N. Conference on Environment and Development. We have deep reservations about...the Law of the Sea Treaty. We emphatically reject U.N. Agenda 21,...and we oppose any form of Global Tax." (Page 51)

"The Republican Party does not accept the jurisdiction of the International Criminal Court. Our service members must be subject only to American law." (Page 51)

"Radical Islamic terrorism poses an existential threat to personal freedom and peace around the world. The Republican Party stands united with all victims of terrorism and will fight at home and abroad to destroy terrorist organizations and protect the lives and fundamental liberties of all people." (Page 52)"

THE DEMOCRAT PARTY PLATFORM

"And we will urge U.S. ratification of the Convention on the Elimination of all Forms of Discrimination Against Women." (Page 19)

"And we will continue to fight for ratification of the Convention on the Rights of Persons with Disabilities." (Page 19)

"We support the nuclear agreement with Iran because, as it is vigorously enforced and implemented, it verifiably cuts off all of Iran's pathways to a bomb without resorting to war." (Page 43)

"Democrats will protect our industry, infrastructure, and government from cyberattacks." (Page 44)

"We will work to end the epidemic of gender-based violence around the world. We will urge ratification of the Convention for the Elimination of all Forms of Discrimination Against Women." (Page 46)

"Democrats believe that global institutions—most prominently the United Nations—and multilateral organizations have a powerful role to play and are an important amplifier of American strength and influence." (Page 51)"

STATEMENTS ABOUT ISRAEL

THE REPUBLICAN PARTY PLATFORM

"We recognize Jerusalem as the eternal and indivisible capital of the Jewish state and call for the American embassy to be moved there in fulfillment of U.S. law. We reaffirm America's commitment to Israel's security and will ensure that Israel maintains a qualitative military edge over any and all adversaries. We reject the false notion that Israel is an occupier and specifically recognize that the Boycott, Divestment, and Sanctions Movement (BDS) is anti-Semitic in nature and seeks to destroy Israel." (Page 47)

The Democrat Party Platform

"A strong Israel is vital to the United States...we will always support Israel's right to defend itself, including by retaining its qualitative military edge, and oppose any effort to delegitimize Israel, including at the United Nations or through the Boycott, Divestment, and Sanctions Movement. We will continue to work toward a two-state solution of the Israeli-Palestinian conflict.... (Page 49) While Jerusalem is a matter for final status negotiations, it should remain the capital of Israel, an undivided city." (Page 50)

Statements about the Military

The Republican Party Platform

"... the Republican Party is committed to rebuilding the U.S. military into the strongest on earth, with vast superiority over any other nation or group of nations in the world." (Page 41)

"We oppose the reinstatement of the draft, except in dire circumstances like world war, whether directly or through compulsory national service. We reiterate our support for both the advancement of women in the military and their exemption from direct ground combat units and infantry battalions." (Page 43)

"America has a sacred trust with our veterans, and we are committed to ensuring them and their families' care and dignity." (Page 44) That includes allowing veterans to choose to access care in the community and not just in VA facilities, because the best care in the world is not effective if it is not accessible." (Page 45)

The Democrat Party Platform

"We believe our military should be the best-trained, best equipped fighting force in the world, and that we must do everything we can to honor and support our veterans. And we know that only the United States can mobilize common action on a truly global scale, to take on the challenges that transcend borders, from international terrorism to climate change to health pandemics." (Page 2)

"We are proud of the repeal of Don't Ask, Don't Tell, and we commit ourselves to insuring fair treatment for LGBT veterans, including by proactively reviewing and upgrading discharge records for veterans who were discharged because of their sexual orientation. Our military is strongest when people of all races, religions, sexual orientations, and gender identities are honored for their service to our country." (Page 41)

"Democrats will seek an updated Authorization for Use of Military Force…that is more precise about our efforts to defeat ISIS and that does not involve large-scale combat deployment of American troops." (Page 42)

"We will strengthen the (Non-Proliferation of Nuclear Weapons) push for the ratification of the Comprehensive Nuclear-Test-Ban Treaty and stop the spread of loose nuclear material…be informed by a new Nuclear Posture Review…with the aim of reducing our reliance on nuclear weapons while meeting our national security obligations." (Page 44)

"Climate change poses an urgent and severe threat to our national security,…. According to the military, climate change is a threat multiplier that is already contributing to new conflicts." (Page 45)"

STATEMENTS ABOUT IMMIGRATION

THE REPUBLICAN PARTY PLATFORM
"Our immigration system must protect American working families and their wages, for citizens and legal immigrants alike, in a way that will improve the economy." (Page 25)

"We oppose any form of amnesty for those who, by breaking the law, have disadvantaged those who have obeyed it." (Page 25)

"… we support stiffer penalties, such as a mandatory minimum sentence of five years, for any illegal alien who illegally re-enters our nation after already having been deported." (Page 26)

"Because 'sanctuary cities' violate federal law and endanger their own citizens, they should not be eligible for federal funding." (Page 26)

"To ensure our national security, refugees who cannot be carefully vetted cannot be admitted to the country...." (Page 26)

"To keep our people safe, we must secure our borders, enforce our immigration laws, and properly screen refugees and other immigrants entering from any country." (Page 42)

THE DEMOCRAT PARTY PLATFORM

"Democrats believe we need to urgently fix our broken immigration system...and create a path to citizenship for law-abiding families..." (Page 17)

"...we will defend and implement President Obama's Deferred Action for Childhood Arrivals and Deferred Action of Parents of Americans executive actions to help DREAMers, parents of citizens, and lawful permanent resident avoid deportation." (Page 17)

"We will work to ensure that all Americans—regardless of immigration status—have access to quality health care. That means expanding community health centers...." (Page 18)

"Given the immense human suffering in Syria, it is also imperative that we lead the international community in providing greater humanitarian assistance to the civilian victims of war in Syria and Iraq, especially displaced refugees." (Page 42)

STATEMENTS ABOUT GUN CONTROL

THE REPUBLICAN PARTY PLATFORM

"We support firearm reciprocity legislation to recognize the right of law-abiding Americans to carry firearms to protect themselves and their families in all 50 states. We also oppose any effort to deprive individuals of their right to keep and bear arms without due process of law." (Page 12)

THE DEMOCRAT PARTY PLATFORM

"With 33,000 Americans dying every year, Democrats believe that we must finally take sensible action to address gun violence...we will expand and strengthen background check and close dangerous loopholes in our current laws; repeal the Protection of Lawful Commerce in Arms Act (PLCAA) to revoke the dangerous legal immunity protections gun makers and sellers now enjoy; and keep weapons of war—such as assault weapons and large capacity ammunition magazines...off our streets." (Page 39)"

STATEMENTS ABOUT FISCAL RESPONSIBILITY

THE REPUBLICAN PARTY PLATFORM

"Republicans consider the establishment of a pro-growth tax code a moral imperative." (Page 1)

"To guard against hyper-taxation of the American people in any restructuring of the federal tax system, any value added tax or national sales tax must be tied to the simultaneous repeal of the Sixteenth Amendment, which established the federal income tax." (Page 2)

"We propose to level the international playing field by lowering the corporate tax rate to be on a par with, or below, the rates of other industrial nations." (Page 2)

"We cannot allow foreign governments to limit American access to their markets while stealing our designs, patents, brands, know-how, and technology." (Page 2)

"In response to the financial institutions crisis of 2008-2009, the... Congress enacted...known as Dodd-Frank...to establish unprecedented government control over the nation's financial markets...the (Consumer Financial Protection) Bureau...should be subjected to congressional appropriation." (Page 3)

"Minimum wage is an issue that should be handled at the state and local level." (Page 8)

"We must impose firm caps on future debt...spending restraint is a necessary component that must be vigorously pursued." (Page 8)

"The Republican path to fiscal sanity and economic expansion begins with a constitutional requirement for a federal balanced budget." (Page 23)

THE DEMOCRAT PARTY PLATFORM

"We believe that today's extreme level of income and wealth inequality—where the majority of the economic gains go to the top one percent... makes our economy weaker, our communities poorer, and our politics poisonous." (Page 1)

"We believe that Americans should earn at least $15 an hour and have the right to form or join a union..." (Page 3)

"We will increase investments to make quality childcare more affordable, boost wages for childcare workers, and support the millions of people paying for, coordinating, or providing care for aging relatives or those with disabilities." (Page 5)

"We will preserve and increase the supply of affordable rental housing by expanding incentives to ease local barriers to building new affordable rental housing developments in areas of economic opportunity." (Page 5)

"And we will fight for robust funding to end homelessness in our cities and counties once and for all..." (Page 6)

"Democrats will expand Social Security.... We will fight every effort to cut, privatize, or weaken Social Security, including attempts to raise the retirement age, diminish benefits by cutting cost-of-living adjustments, or reducing earned benefits...by asking those at the top to pay more... by taxing some of the income of people above $250,000." (Page 6)

"We will also vigorously implement, enforce, and build on President Obama's landmark Dodd-Frank financial reform law, and we will stop dead in its tracks every Republican effort to weaken it." (Page 11)

"We support a financial transactions tax on Wall Street to curb excessive speculation and high-frequency trading…." (Page 11)

"At a time of massive income and wealth inequality, we believe the wealthiest Americans and largest corporations must pay their fair share of taxes." (Page 12)

"We will ensure those at the top contribute to our country's future by establishing a multimillionaire surtax to ensure millionaires and billionaires pay their fair share…restore fair taxation on multi-million dollar estates…." (Page 13)

"Democrats believe that we need to give Americans affordable banking options, including by empowering the United States Postal Service to facilitate the delivery of basic banking services." (Page 12)

"Disparities in wealth cannot be solved by the free market alone, but instead, the federal government must play a role in eliminating systemic barriers to wealth accumulation." (Page 15)

"Because of conflicting federal and state laws concerning marijuana, we encourage the federal government to remove marijuana from the list of 'Schedule 1' controlled substances…providing a reasoned pathway for future legalization." (Page 16)

"We will remove barriers to help formerly incarcerated individuals successfully re-enter society by 'banning the box,' (indicating criminal records), expanding reentry programs, and restoring voting rights…." (Page 16)

"We will continue to support the Violence Against Women Act to provide law enforcement with the tools it needs to combat this problem." (Page 38)

Statements about Election and Campaign laws

The Republican Party Platform
"We support legislation to require proof of citizenship when registering to vote and secure photo ID when voting." (Page 16)

"We urge our elected representatives to ensure that citizenship rather than mere residency, be made the basis for the apportionment of representatives among the states." (Page 16)"

The Democrat Party Platform
"Democrats believe we are stronger when we protect citizens' right to vote, while stopping corporations' out-sized influence in elections. ... restore the full power of the Voting Rights Act." (Page 2)

"We must rectify the Supreme Court decision gutting the Voting Rights Act, which is a profound injustice. We will stop efforts by Republican governors and legislatures to disenfranchise people of color, low-income people, and young people, and prevent these voters from exercising their right to vote through onerous restrictions." (Page 24)

"We will bring our democracy into the 21st century by expanding early voting and vote-by-mail, implementing universal automatic voter registration and same day voter registration, ending partisan and racial gerrymandering and making Election Day a national holiday." (Page 24)

"Democrats support a constitutional amendment to overturn the Supreme Court's decisions in *Citizens United and Buckley v. Valeo.* We need to end secret, unaccountable money in politics by requiring, through executive order or legislation, significantly more disclosure and transparency." (Page 25)

"We will preserve and enhance the integrity and accuracy of the census and the American Community Survey (ACS)…improve counting segments of the population…persistently undercounted, specifically communities of color, immigrants, LBGT people, young children, those with disabilities, and rural and low-income populations." (Page 26)

CHAPTER 13

PRAYER OF VISION & PASSION

God led America's pilgrims to a new land called America much like He led Abraham. America's early settlers believed, "This land is His land."

After enduring a voyage of 65, days the ship reached the shores of Cape Cod, in the cold month of November.

With grateful hearts and strong hands, they blazed a new way of life. They were people of prayer who knew God was providing the means for them to occupy the land where He had led them.

America has developed and changed a lot since the Pilgrims arrived, but God has not changed his plan for America. In every generation, He has raised up new believers whom He has chosen to occupy the land and share His story. His message is, "I have come that they might have life, and that they may have *it* more abundantly" (John 10:10 NKJV).

The Constitution and Bill of Rights alone cannot keep America safe. It is the people who believe, pray, and trust him in every generation that He uses to make America strong.

President Ronald Reagan said, "Freedom is a fragile thing and is never more than one generation away from extinction. It is not ours by inheritance; it must be fought for and defended constantly by each generation."

The reality is many Americans have moved from independence of government to dependency and entitlement. Churches are being forced to pay for abortions. Pastors are being forced to perform same-sex marriages and are being subpoenaed for preaching Truth. Flags are burned, and protesters gather on the steps of state capitol building, shouting, shout, "Kill the infidels."

We are being hammered and consumed by egregious violations of our fundamental human rights and constitutionally protected freedoms.

Yet, the love of Jesus equips us to occupy this land where He has placed us. We are not here by accident. As we are planted in America's love fields, we are to both kneel before Him and stand with Him.

His direction for us is to go daily to the foot of the cross and pick up our cross and follow him. His cross is not just an instrument death; it is a bridge of life. It is empty because his love plan is finished, and we can't add anything to it. (See Matthew 16:34.)

Jesus has chosen us to occupy our place of grace where He has planted us. (See John 15:16.) What does it mean?

When Jesus gave us a new heart, He set us free to live an empowered life. "His divine power has given us everything we need for a godly life through our knowledge of him who called us by his own glory and goodness" (2 Peter 1:3 NIV).

As citizens of our beloved nation, we are to so live that people can look at us — look at our love, look at our lifestyle — and see a picture of God's love and might as we march in God's love parade.

Are you ready to get out of the closet of tears and fears and report for love duty? If you are ready, let's pray:

Lord, I pray for the power of your Holy Spirit to move among us in America as we start a new era with new national leaders. We live in a diverse nation with people of many faiths and colors. We ask that you heal the wounded warriors and restore mutual respect and honor to our government.

I ask for forgiveness for not just the things we have done that are not right, but for the things we have not done that are right. Lord, help me to be an ambassador for freedom and unity. I reject the cynical and crippling spirit that the Enemy of Easter has poured out in the hearts of your people. I ask you to use you Holy scanner to show us your plan and passion for freedom.

Lord, I pray that the leaders that America has chosen will fall on their knees and trust you for life, liberty and freedom. I pray that those who refuse to do that will be removed and replaced with people of integrity, intelligence and inspiration who trust in You.

Lord, give our leaders wisdom, vision, passion and inspiration as they follow you. Guide and instruct them in making laws that fit your plans for good and not evil. Above all things Lord, may all of our elected leaders search their hearts and follow, serve and please you. Guide all of us and bless us that all can look at us and see You. Amen

Unit 7

America's Leaders Report for Duty

Time to Praise & Pray for America

John Bornschein

A Time to Pray

"...if my people who are called by my name, will humble
themselves and pray and seek my face and turn from their wicked
ways, then will I hear from heaven and will forgive their sin and will
heal their land" (2 Chronicles 7:14 HCSB).

Second Chronicles 7:14 contains a remarkable promise from the
Almighty God that speaks of forgiveness and healing for nations
and for believers. But as awesome a prophetic promise as it is for
America, many believers forget that it is a conditional promise.
When believers meet His conditions, God will honor His promise.

As we look at this country, we see a nation that is morally
bankrupt and in spiritual decline. Vulgarity, indecency, obscenities,
lies, and corruption are today's norm. Economic struggles, terrorist
threats, sexual immorality, and the breakdown of families are just
a few problems our country faces. We are a fractured people and
nation, and we need healing through God's divine intervention.

If My People, Who Are Called by My Name

The solutions to the nation's problems lie not with politicians,
reformers, educators, or business leaders, but with God's people.
Today, God's people are those who worship Him, who accept and
follow the Lord Jesus Christ as Lord and Savior – men and women
who are His, not just in name, but in every aspect of their lives. In
the darkest of situations, the Church can call out to God, and He
will hear. This promise has not expired, but remains the key that
makes it possible for all His people to take full responsibility for our
condition and turn back the spiritual decline.

68

In fact, God has given the Church four conditions to seeing His healing come to our nation and our lives, and they are all centered in changes that take place in our hearts.

WILL HUMBLE THEMSELVES

Humility means "to bend the knee, to bow down, to be in subjection to." Humility is when we truly understand how poor and needy we are before God. Those who are humble know what it means to grieve over their sins and the sins of others. Simply put, humility means we are utterly dependent on God, which is the opposite of pride. James 4:16 tells us that "God opposes the proud but gives grace to the humble."

Being humble is a difficult position, because we all tend to depend on any number of other factors than God only, whether it is our education, our career, our accomplishments and works, or our spiritual résumé. Both individually and as a Church there is a need to set aside our pride and humble ourselves. We must be willing to get on our faces before God, come to the cross of Christ with nothing but ourselves, and cry out to Him for a fresh outpouring of His Holy Spirit on our lives and out to the world.

AND PRAY

To pray means to "ask" when you want God to do something for you and for others. The sovereign God has ordained prayer as the tool to get His work done, and He works in accord with the praying of His people and His own sovereign will. Prayer not only prepares us to do His work, but it is the work that must be done before any other work for the Lord is done. However, we in the Church tend to do almost anything but pray and often treat prayers as though it is a last resort rather than the first thing we should do. We as individuals and the Church must pray. All the major revivals have come because of believers who were serious enough to cry out to God in prayer.

AND SEEK MY FACE

God has said, "You will seek me and find me when you seek me with all your heart" (Jeremiah 29:13 NIV). God is personal, and we must deal with Him as a person. Too often, we seek the hand of God, which represents His works, instead of the face of God, which represents His nature and who He really is. When we seek His face, we see His holiness and love, which exposes our sin and depravity and selfishness. When we seek His face, we come with adoration and praise and worship, and we are changed and want to love Him more dearly and walk with Him more intimately. When we seek His face, we begin to hear His voice and discover His love and mercy that pardon us of all our sins.

And Turn From Their Wicked Ways

The psalmist said, "If I had cherished sin in my heart, the Lord would not have listened" (Psalm 66:18 NIV). If we want to experience the presence of God that changes our lives and the world, we need to get rid of anything that pushes Christ from the center of our lives. It might be our complacency, apathy, and indifference to what God is concerned about – the poor, the brokenhearted, the exploited, or the unemployed. God hates sin and all forms of wickedness, whether it is abortion, sexual sins, lying, cheating, drunkenness, drug abuse, hatred, jealousy, envy, and fits of rage. And He is not pleased with a Church that refuses to stand out against the many great evils of our day – believers who never fight for what is right, who compromise in an attempt not to offend, who carry no cross and stand for nothing.

Then Will I Hear from Heaven and Will Forgive Their Sin and Will Heal Their Land

From the place of authority, heaven itself, God will "hear," which means "to listen to a point where you are moved to action." In other words, He has promised to respond to their prayers. Evangelist Dwight L. Moody said that when God's people fulfill His conditions, He "brings heaven within speaking distance."

Standing by Faith

Usually Satan will try to suggest to you that your prayers were not heard. He will encourage you to look to the problems again and get your eyes off God. He will try to get you to talk as if you are not sure if your prayer is answered. Charles Cowman said, "The devil is not put to flight by a courteous request. He meets us at every turn, contends for every inch, and our progress has to be registered in heart's blood and tears."

Be prepared for warfare with Satan. Take firm control of your thought life. Think on positive things. (See Philippians 4:6-9.) By praising God and confessing the relevant truths of the Word, cast down every thought that is contrary to your prayer. Keep speaking what the Word of God says on the issue at stake. "Let us hold unswervingly to the hope we profess, for he who promised is faithful" (Hebrews 10:23 NIV). Then, keep believing you will see your prayers answered.

Never lose sight of the fact that there may be specific reasons why a prayer is not answered immediately. God may desire that your faith be exercised and strengthened through your patient waiting on Him. Settle it in your mind that God is always true and faithful to His promises. It may be that your heart is not prepared for the answer to your prayer, but it is on the way.

Praying Like Jesus

Anne Graham Lotz

It's been said that the only thing necessary for the triumph of evil is for good men to do nothing. The encroaching evil in our land is almost breathtaking. Heart-stopping. As it pours into every nook and cranny of our culture, it is also going to be life-altering and life-shattering.

What can the righteous do? "When the foundations are being destroyed, what can the righteous do?" (Psalm 11:3 NIV).

As I've read reports of shootings in Louisiana and Minnesota.... as I've shared the agony of a nation that is reeling from the cold-blooded, deliberate, pre-planned murder of police officers...as I've watched the eruption of anarchy in the streets...as I've wept with grief almost deeper than words but expressed by a silent scream in my heart...I've asked the Lord, *What are we to do? Is there anything ordinary, good people can do?*

As I waited in prayer, four things came to my mind:

We are to pray. Paul challenges us, "With this in mind, be alert and always keep on praying" (Ephesians 6:18 NIV). It's time for you and me to establish a set-aside time of consistent, daily prayer. Just give us Jesus.

Pick up the sword of the Spirit which is the word of God, (See Ephesians 6:17.). This is a time to daily, consistently spend time in God's Word, strengthening the foundation of our faith as we listen to what God has to say. But don't just read it. Apply it. Obey it. Live it out.

Pursue righteousness. (See 2 Timothy 2:22-24.) Pursue the right thing, not necessarily the popular or the politically correct thing. Stand up for justice, truth, kindness and love...by our own example.

Proclaim Jesus. Be ready at a moment's notice to share the Gospel and give a reason for the Hope that is within you.

Please, don't just do nothing. Do something! What can we do?

> Pray just give me Jesus
>
> Pick up your sword.
>
> Pursue righteousness.
>
> Proclaim Jesus until He comes.

Freedom for Praising

Dr. Steve Washburn

Freedom is a beautiful thing. A precious thing. A fragile thing. An extremely costly thing. We've always been free.

We're as comfortable in our freedom as we are in a well-worn pair of blue jeans. In fact, we may be taking our freedom for granted. Freedom should be appreciated and celebrated.

Paul said, "Christ has liberated us to be free. Stand firm then and don't submit again to a yoke of slavery. ... For you are called to be free, brothers; only don't use this freedom as an opportunity for the flesh, but serve one another through love" (Galatians 5:1, 13 HCSB).

Let's always celebrate our *freedom of religion*. In this passage Paul is primarily talking about freedom from Judaism. But the concept he describes applies to all freedom of religion.

In 1534, England broke ties with the Roman Catholic Church and started their own religion, called the Church of England. A group within the Church of England wanted to take advantage of the split and "purify" the new religion from all Catholic influences. They were appropriately called "Puritans". Some of these Puritans, however, saw little progress in purifying the religion, and decided to "separate" completely from England's church. They were called "Separatists", or "Pilgrims". Since the King of England controlled the Church of England, the Pilgrims were considered treasonous. They lived in danger of persecution, and even imprisonment. So in 1607, they left England.[1] For 10 years they lived in Holland. But in Holland their children were influenced by the perverse immoral culture there (much like here today).[2] So in 1620, they joined a London stock company that financed their trip to America aboard the Mayflower. They intended to join the Virginia Company that had been chartered by King James, the new King of England.[3] But they were blown off course and landed in what is today Plymouth, Mass.

So The Pilgrims came here, and established the Plymouth colony, and became the foundation of the United States of America, primarily for two reasons: 1) To find freedom of religion from strong state pressure, and, 2) to deliver their children from perverse immoral influences.

Does any of that sound familiar? As we separate ourselves from the doctrines being spread by our culture, are we being pressured and persecuted? Absolutely! And are our children being indoctrinated and influenced into this culture's perverse immorality? Of course they are!

The similarities between our situation and that of our pilgrim ancestors are obvious. Except we have no distant new world to which to run. Although shrinking, we must not take our remaining freedom of religion for granted. Let's celebrate our freedom of religion and do all we can to sustain it.

Let's also celebrate our *freedom from tyranny*. By 1776 our ancestors had escaped the forced religion of England, but were still under the forced tyranny of England.

Scripture verses like Galatians 5:1 & 13 echoed in the hearts and minds of our founding fathers, most of whom were serious followers of Christ Jesus. Freedom from tyranny burned deep and hot in their hearts.

Mendell Taylor quotes one early source this way:

"The Declaration of Independence is not only one of the world's great political documents: it is also, and primarily, a religious Magna Carta - written and signed by men to whom religion was all-important as the basis of lasting freedom. Its glowing principles were written 'with a firm reliance upon the protection of divine Providence.' Among the fifty-six signers, none was an unbeliever... Before they strode forward to append their signatures, each man bowed his head in prayer".[4]

That Declaration of Independence from tyranny was born in the Bible of Christ and birthed by followers of Christ.

Let's remember that freedom from tyranny was *declared by the courage of patriots* - primarily because of convictions revealed to them in Scripture. And then freedom from tyranny was *purchased by the blood of patriots* - very similar to the way freedom from tyranny of sin was purchased by the blood of Jesus. And then finally, freedom from tyranny continues to be *sustained by the blood of patriots* – because freedom is always a very costly thing.

American Demographics did a survey asking the question, "How well does the word 'patriotic' describe you?" Among participants above 60, 77% said they would describe themselves as patriotic. Among participants between ages 50 and 59, 67% described themselves as patriots. Between ages 35 and 49 only 44% said they were patriotic. That's a 30-point decrease. But here's what is concerning: Among millennials, ages 18 to 34, just 35% describe themselves as patriotic. Two thirds of individuals between 18-34 see little or no value in patriotism!

Katherine Floyd tells of one of her students, a boy named Luigi, a first generation American. During their study of American history, as she explained the great personal price the signers of the Declaration of Independence had to pay, she passed around a copy of the document. When it came to Luigi, he looked at it very carefully, and then, in an almost reverent manner, he signed his own name to the bottom of the list of signatures.[5]

That is the spirit of a patriot! Not afraid. Not ashamed. Not confused. Willing and ready to pay the price to sustain our freedom from tyranny.

And finally, let's celebrate our *freedom in Christ.* The central theme that so heavily influences this discussion of freedom – is *Jesus!* Jesus is the source of all true freedom. After describing Himself as God's "Truth", Jesus said in John 8:32, "*You will know the Truth and the Truth will set you free.*"

And the thing that has gotten so hopelessly lost over the last five decades is that our founding fathers recognized this. Jesus, and the teachings of Jesus are reflected in The Declaration of Independence, the Constitution, the Bill of Rights, and the writings and quotes and offices held by our founding fathers. All of it built on the instructions of Jesus.

So what has happened? Toward the close of the Civil War, Abe Lincoln spoke to the slaves he had just freed: "My poor friends, you are free-free as air. You can cast off the name of slave and trample upon it. Liberty is your birth-right... Now don't let your joy carry you into excesses. Learn the laws and follow them." There! That's what happened.

We've allowed the joys of our freedom to carry us into excesses, and we've stopped following Christ's instructions.

Catholic priest and author Francis Canavan wrote:

> We did away with state churches in this country so that all Protestants could feel at home in it. We de-Protestantized the country so that Catholics, too, could feel at home in it. We have dechristianized the country to make Jews feel welcome, and then dereligionized it so that atheists and agnostics may feel equally welcome. Now we are demoralzing the country so that deviants from accepted moral norms will not feel excluded. The lowest common denominator, we have discovered, is like the horizon, always approached but never reached.[6]

True freedom is not found in the lowest common denominator. True freedom is found where it has always been found - in following Christ. Let us celebrate our freedom in Christ by nudging our nation back toward the teachings of Christ.

Preparing Your Heart for Praise

Gerry Wakeland

Recently my pastor shared this quote "Everyone is either in the midst of a crisis, just coming out of a crisis, or getting ready to enter into a crisis." How true that is. I speak from personal experience. My life has seen a number of crises over the years. Perhaps that's why this verse from 1 Kings is so meaningful to me.

"A hurricane wind ripped through the mountains and shattered the rocks before God, but God wasn't to be found in the wind; after the wind an earthquake, but God wasn't in the earthquake; and after the earthquake fire, but God wasn't in the fire; and after the fire a gentle and quiet whisper" (1 Kings 19:11-12 The Message).

As a child I spent a great deal of time in church. We went to Sunday School and then sat with my parents in the "big" church. On Sunday night we had Bible study and there were always activities during the week. We did it all. However, I didn't always understand the lessons being taught. There was a lot that went right over my head.

Good Friday 1964 was a day I'll never forget. My parents were attending Good Friday services and my sister and I were having dinner with friends. We had just sat down to eat our spaghetti when Anchorage, Alaska where we lived was hit with a 9.2 magnitude earthquake. I thought the world was coming to an end. In some ways it was. My father's job was impacted and that summer we moved. The transition was difficult for a 10-year old child. I did not see God in the earthquake.

January 11, 1968 was another day that will stay etched in my memory forever. We were now living on a 40-acre farm just outside Marion, IL. My mother had taken me to a neighboring town for an appointment with an orthopedic surgeon. Through a series of events we never saw the surgeon that day. Instead six hours later we were sent home.

From the end of the country road we could see the smoke. My mother drove up the hill just as fast as our little old Pontiac would go. As we crossed over the railroad tracks it became obvious that our house was on fire. My sister was standing in the front yard. No cell phones to reach for, instead we turned around and raced back down the hill to the nearest neighbor's home only to discover they had already called the fire department. The firefighters arrived and sadly told us there was nothing they could do. Our well, the only water source, was too close to the fire and they could not access the water safely. They also confirmed what we had tried to deny as long as possible. My father had been trapped in the fire and did not make it out. I can still hear the ticking of the grandfather clock in the parlor of the funeral home as we sat and waited for my mother to make arrangements. A few years older now, I did not see God in the fire.

Growing up without a father was challenging. I made a lot of poor decisions. There were many times that I could not find God anywhere. But by now I was not really looking.

I got married while I was still in high school. You might say I was trying to escape. After the birth of my two girls, it was obvious that the marriage was not going to work. After my divorce, I married a man that moved our family to Southern California where I continued my nomadic journey in the spiritual wilderness.

If you recall the story of Moses found in Exodus 2-3, God allowed Moses to escape to Midian and "hide-out" serving as a shepherd for his father-in-law. But that lasted just so long until one day God got Moses' attention. He spoke to him from a burning bush.

I did not have an actual burning bush experience but the day came when I realized that I was about to lose everything I held dear, and God got my attention. I made my way out of the wilderness and back into the arms of God. I knew God had something for me to do so I waited and listened and all the while I served the Lord, whatever He asked, wherever He sent me. The waiting room God had me in was like an incubator of learning. Or maybe you might say remembering because a lot of those lessons I learned as a child in church started coming back. All those Scriptures I memorized, all the words to the many old hymns I sang, suddenly I could remember them all. God was preparing me for something, I had no idea what.

In the fall of 1999, my husband retired and we moved back to Central Illinois. Less than six months later he was diagnosed with stage four throat cancer. Once more my world was turned upside down. Isaiah 55:8-9 reads, "For my thoughts are not your thoughts, neither are your ways my ways," declares the LORD. As the heavens are higher than the earth, so are my ways higher than your ways and my thoughts than your thoughts" (NIV). And for the next seven months He proved this to me over and over again.

They say that you are never really ready to lose a loved one and I heartily agree, but I do believe that God helps you prepare. As hard as it was to watch my husband draw his last breath, I could do so with great thanksgiving, praising God for His mercy and grace.

You might be wondering, "How could she do that?" How can you praise God in the trials and tribulations, in the crises of life? You have to prepare your heart to praise Him, no matter the situation or circumstances. He is a God that deserves our praise.

How do you prepare your heart? Let me share three ways that have worked for me, even when I was not aware of it.

YOU HAVE TO PRACTICE

Nothing worthwhile ever comes easy. You have to practice. I have always wanted to play the piano well. I just didn't want to practice. You can learn to praise Him – always. Start practicing now. When you practice praise, He gets your heart ready for the next best thing.

YOU HAVE TO PUSH

Some years ago, I was teaching a class on prayer and during our discussion time one of the participants told us we have to push. That seemed strange so I asked her to explain. She said you have to pray until something happens, push. The same is true about praise. You have to praise until something happens, push. Whether you feel like it or not, just praise Him. If you don't know how, start by reading the Psalms. Read them out loud. Read them over and over again.

YOU HAVE TO PERSEVERE

Winston Churchill said, "Never, never, never, give up." This is so true. When I was in the worst possible place and had praised and praised and praised and nothing was changing, I was ready to throw in the towel. I was tired and defeated. That's just what the enemy wants. John 10:10 tells us that the thief comes to only to steal and kill and destroy. Don't let him take what God has for you. Keep praising. Expect a breakthrough. It's coming.

I encourage you to begin now to prepare your heart to praise Jesus . When trouble comes you will be ready. You may not hear Him in the wind, or the earthquake, or even the fire. But you will hear Him in your praises and He will hear you and bless you.

Rain, Revival, and Rejoicing

Dr. Trey Kent

No man is greater than his prayer life and no city or nation will rise above the prayers of God's people. These are challenging words. How blessed do you want our nation to be? I know you are reading this because you have a heart to join me and millions of others to cry out for a changed America!

In February of 2008, I was awakened to the world of prayer like never before. My wife and I were on a prayer walk at 12:30 am in our town of Cedar Park, Texas, a suburb of Austin, when God spoke to me saying: "Wouldn't it be wonderful if 31 churches would adopt one day of prayer every month and My city could be covered in prayer 24 hours a day, 365 days a year?" That encounter changed my life. I now realize one of my primary callings is praying for the greater Austin area and to mobilize God's church to pray for revival 24/7. Since that day we have mobilized 50 churches who are praying night and day. Austin has been covered with 24/7 prayer since 2009.

> "When I shut up the heavens so that there is no rain, or command the locust to devour the land, or send pestilence among my people, if my people who are called by my name humble themselves, and pray and seek my face and turn from their wicked ways, then I will hear from heaven and will forgive their sin and heal their land"
> (2 Chronicles 7:13-14 NKJV).

On September 20, 2013, the Austin area was at the peak of a major drought. Lake Travis, our area water source, was at a 50 year low of 618 feet. That's 63 feet below full. The experts were saying that there was no hope in sight and that Lake Travis would be a dust bowl in the next 20 years. That's when the pastors and prayer warriors in Austin awoke to our need to cry out in keeping with 2 Chronicles 7:14. It was our responsibility to cry out when there is no rain. We are called to humble ourselves, pray, seek God's face, and turn from our wicked ways. If we do these things, it's God's promise that He will hear our prayers, forgive our sin, and heal our land! This is our sure promise from the Lord!

Because of the lingering drought and loss of hope, Austin area pastors called a day of prayer for *rain* and *revival*. On May 22, 2014, a thousand believers from across our city came together at Hyde Park Baptist Church and cried out for rain; we humbled ourselves seeking revival. Our battle cry was 681—that the number of the feet of water we would need for a full lake. The next day it began to rain. And month after month, we began to see the lake rise little by little. Then, in May 2015, in a one-month period, the lake rose 32 feet. And finally in March 2016, Lake Travis reached a full 681 feet. And to make our prayer miracle even more amazing, that day was exactly 681 days from our first prayer meeting for rain until our second prayer meeting to rejoice in a full lake. What an amazing God. Our God answers prayer!

Rain

The lack of rain was a sign we needed to pray. Our nation's woes, crime, division, poverty, hatred, godlessness, and all, show that we as God's people must take our stand in prayer together for God to heal our land. It was an amazing realization that the lack of rain was a call for us to pray. The dilemmas of our day are warning signs, alarms so to speak, calling us to intercede for breakthrough in America. What if God gave us what we asked for? What would come to America because of your prayers?

Revival

To see transforming revival is the goal of our lives. Most people never realize the reason we were created is to know God and to see His will done on earth as it is in heaven. Revival, the filling of the earth with the glory of God, is God's will for this earth. One simple definition of revival is to see masses of people turn to "love God with all their hearts, souls, minds and strength and to love their neighbor as themselves." This is what we are called to give ourselves to in this life. Why not stop right here, right now and pray about giving yourself to see revival in your life, in your family, in your church, neighborhood, nation and world?

REJOICING

True joy is what occurs as we fall deeper in love with Jesus. The more deeply we experience His love, the deeper the joy we experience. After God answered our prayer for rain we had a great service of celebration—rejoicing in a God who answers prayer. Have you stopped recently to rejoice in God and say "thank you?" Most of us are live like the nine lepers Jesus healed, we never stop to say thanks. There is a joy in God that sets us apart from all peoples on the earth. Our family, friends and acquaintances must see a powerful joy exuding from our lives. Stop now and say thanks and ask God to give you His greater joy as you know and serve him more.

PRAYING FOR AMERICA

Let's conclude with a clear guide to pray for America. America's greatest need is a true and living relationship with Jesus Christ! And, nothing will get us there faster than God's people crying out in prayer.

PRAYER GUIDE FOR AMERICA

✝ **A**-sk God to heal our land as we humble ourselves, pray, seek His face, and turn from our wicked ways.

✝ **M**-eekly admit that we are in desperate need as a nation for revival and a healed land.

✝ **E**-agerly say thanks for all God's blessings on you, your family and our nation.

✝ **R**-epent of your sins and the sins of our nation. Be as specific as possible.

✝ **I**-ntercede for Jesus to reveal Himself to our nation once again.

✝ **C**-ry out to God for mercy upon our sinful land.

✝ **A**-sk for God to revive His church and use the revived church to reach our nation for Christ.

Now can be our finest hour. God responds to a praying people. Every revival in the history of the world resulted from united prayer. I urge you to begin praying today and to mobilize two or three others who can pray with you for God to bring revival. We must bring our lives into agreement with God's purposes on the earth. Remember, the darker it is, the brighter the light of Jesus will shine in our nation. God is not finished with America, and we are His watchman on the wall who are called to cry out day and night for a revived America.

Let's remember God's amazing promise.

And will not God give justice to his elect, who cry to him day and night? Will he delay long over them? I tell you, he will give justice to them speedily (Luke 18:7 HCSB).

POWER OF PRAISE FOR LIFE

CAROL EVERETT

I am an American, a woman, a mother, a grandmother—and a woman who took the life of her own daughter.

Instantly, I knew I had murdered my unborn child. People said I had made the right decision to have an abortion—so "I" must be the problem. I stuffed those feelings, and then desperately attempted to justify my sin by selling abortions to other girls and women. Each time I sold an abortion, in some twisted way, my own abortion decision became more acceptable.

At that time, the abortion industry was open to women who were hurt by abortion, and it was there I found a way to justify my abortion on a daily basis. My goal was to be a millionaire through selling abortions to others for a $25 commission. To reach this goal, I worked hard to sell 40,000 abortions a year.

During my last eighteen months in the industry, we rushed one injured woman, out of every 500, to the hospital for a hysterectomy or colostomy. One young woman died.

No lawsuits. Why? The shame of abortion protects the abortion industry.

I began to question everything, but moved forward. Then I had an encounter with the Lord of Life, and He affected an instant turnaround in my life. I began to share my life story so others can know the truth about the abortion industry and its goal to sell abortions to children and make them "customers for life."

Rights? Choices? Rape? Incest? Woman's right to choose?

Roe v Wade allowed states to offer a woman the right to privacy to choose abortion in 1973. When confronted with an unplanned pregnancy, statistics prove that even Christ followers consider—and in some cases—choose abortion. What does the Bible say about life? "The thief comes only to steal and kill and destroy. I came that they may have life and have it abundantly" (John 10:10).

God is not silent on life. He commands us to "Choose Life." God addresses the mother, rape, incest and His power for creation: "O Lord, you have searched me and known me! You know when I sit down and when I rise up; you discern my thoughts from afar. You search out my path and my lying down and are acquainted with all my ways. Even before a word is on my tongue, behold, O Lord, you know it altogether. You hem me in, behind and before, and lay your hand upon me. Such knowledge is too wonderful for me; it is high; I cannot attain it. Where shall I go from your Spirit? Or where shall I flee from your presence? If I ascend to heaven, you are there! If I make my bed in Sheol, you are there! If I take the wings of the morning and dwell in the uttermost parts of the sea, even there your hand shall lead me, and your right hand shall hold me. If I say, "Surely the darkness shall cover me, and the light about me be night," even the darkness is not dark to you; the night is bright as the day, for darkness is as light with you" (Psalm 139:1-12 ESV). Are these verses speaking to your heart? God is clear that He knows where you are and your situation.

Because God allowed conception to occur, He has a plan for the baby, the mother, and even the criminal father. Law never punishes a child for the crime or sins of the mother or father. Ending the baby's life does not erase the tragic crime of rape but traumatizes the mother a second time. Some question a young mothers' ability to carry the baby to term. If God has allowed conception, He can handle delivery.

Incest is a terrible crime against a girl or woman. If a baby conceived in incest is aborted, the mother is subjected to the trauma of abortion and returned to the same potential abusive situation—incest.

God's Plan is Always Life

"For you formed my inward parts; you knitted me together in my mother's womb. I praise you, for I am fearfully and wonderfully made. Wonderful are your works; my soul knows it very well. My frame was not hidden from you, when I was being made in secret, intricately woven in the depths of the earth. Your eyes saw my unformed substance; in your book were written, every one of them, the days that were formed for me, when as yet there was none of them" (Psalm 139: 13-16 ESV).

The Word sings of God's power to create. Before God created each of us in our mother's womb, He knew us and created each organ, each blood vessel, every inch of flesh on each of us. He formed us in our mother's womb and the days of our lives were planned or ordained before we were.

For the rights and choices of the mother, if God created your baby, God graciously offers His gift of a new life to you.. Your baby can be a different blood type, a different sex, and is not an extension of your body but a human being created in the image of God by God.

God plans abundant life for each of us. Our gift to Him is praise. "How precious to me are your thoughts, O God! How vast is the sum of them! If I would count them, they are more than the sand. I awake, and I am still with you" (Psalm 139:17 ESV).

The Word also declares that God hates evil. We are directed to, "Hate evil, love good: Establish justice in the gate" (Amos 5:15a ESV).

If we understand evil according to Scripture, we will hate abortion and all ungodliness. How do we establish justice in the gate? "Search me, O God, and know my heart! Try me and know my thoughts! And see if there be any grievous way in me, and lead me in the way everlasting" (Psalm 139:22-24 ESV).

God's Word encourages all Christ followers to ask the Lord to show each of us what role we play in furthering life. What specific gift or talent did He plant in us to be used to save the lives of others physically and eternally, and how will He use us for His glory as we work to establish justice?

Governmental authority determines justice by establishing the laws of the land. Elected officials or appointments by elected officials, such as Justices of the Supreme Court, declared Roe versus Wade as the law of the land. We as Christians have responsibilities as citizens. He has called us to pray for each other, our country, and those in authority who make the decisions that guide our laws.

We praise Him and thank Him for the opportunity to be involved in America's leadership by stewardship of our right and obligation to vote. We must examine each candidate's views, opinions, and positions with a comparison to biblical values and vote accordingly.

If Christians prayerfully vote faith, freedom and life values, this nation will stand for truth and turn back to our God.

As I reconciled my sin of abortion to the Lord, He gave me a new vision for life and a powerful promise.

I named my daughter Heidi. I am blessed in knowing that when I get to heaven, I will hold Heidi for the first time and be able praise the Lord Jesus.

Prayerfully Seeking His Face

Rev. Wayne Winsauer

What is it like to see the face of God? Adam and Eve saw it's light and loved it. Yet they turned their face to the crafty serpent. The temptation, the fall from righteousness, and sin entered into their lives and the lives of all humankind. Suddenly and tragically, darkness covered the earth. God calls the darkness sin.

Jesus is light and love. *The Light shines in the darkness, and the darkness did not comprehend it.* Jesus is the Light of the World. "Jesus again spoke to them, saying, "I am the Light of the world; he who follows Me will not walk in the darkness, but will have the Light of life" (John 1:5 NASU).

What happens when darkness rules? "I will set My face against you so that you will be struck down before your enemies; and those who hate you will rule over you, and you will flee when no one is pursuing you" (Leviticus 25:17 NASU).

The United States of America has lost its way when it comes to God. We are sliding into a time when God is setting His face against us. Americans must make a decision on the direction our nation will take in the days ahead. Each one of us will be affected for good or bad. Without God, those who hate us will rule over us.

Where are you looking?

He is always watching over each one of us. He wants us to seek His face. God has already started to hide His face from us. It a majority of Americans do not care what God thinks, and certainly are not searching for His face.

America needs God

We need Him in our lives.. We must return to God. Repentance is required, then He will show us His face. "Then... He said, 'I will hide

My face from them, I will see what their end shall be; For they are a perverse generation, Sons in whom is no faithfulness'" (Deuteronomy 32:20 NASU).

The Lord hid His face from Israel. Yet there is hope. He says, "I will see what their end shall be" (Deuteronomy 32:20 NASU). God is watching America to see who will turn and seek His face in these days of terror and horror. The verse accuses the people of being perverse. Why not reverse the perverse and walk in the Lord's ways?

Jeremiah 16:17 says, "For My eyes are on all their ways; they are not hidden from My face, nor is their iniquity concealed from My eyes. This is all about Judah's sins. Be assured He is just as able to see our sins. When the day of calamity comes it is too late. God's punishment of America today is undoubtedly well deserved. We as a nation are on the edge of falling apart (NASU).

In Ezekiel 39: 23 "...I hid My face from them; so I gave them into the hand of their adversaries." What happens if God gives us to our adversaries? We will only find mercy when, we as a nation, seek the face of God. Let's hope and pray that it is not too late (NASU).

Isaiah 54:8 "In an outburst of anger I hid My face from you (abandoned) for a moment, but with everlasting lovingkindness I will have compassion on you," Says the LORD your Redeemer." This is about restoration. Here the Lord calls Himself "your Redeemer." Jesus paid the price for you at the cross. He ransomed you from all the evil in your life (NASU).

Does America care? Do you care?' There is hope, and He cares for us. His face will forever be before us and our nation if we praise Him and pray. He promised this to an Old Testament king name King Solomon "....(when) My people who are called by My name humble themselves and pray and seek My face and turn from their wicked ways, then I will hear from heaven, will forgive their sin and will heal their land" (2 Chronicles 7:14 NASU).

As Americans we must humble ourselves, pray and seek His face and turn from our wicked ways. It is then Americans will see the face of God. To continue to hide from his face is to break off communication is revulsion and abhorrence.

WAKE UP AMERICA AND FOCUS

It is time to restore the broken communication line and reestablish contact with Father God. He wants to see our face.

It is not God's fault that many Americans are devoid of spiritual direction. The problem falls squarely on our backs. "Rebellion against God" is sin.

Without the work of the Holy Spirit, America will fail in all that matters. He is the power that holds everything together, and we must ask for the Holy Spirit's help. "But the Helper, the Holy Spirit, whom the Father will send in My name, He will teach you all things, and bring to your remembrance all that I said to you" (John 14:26 NASU).

The Spirit gives life to all by drawing us to Jesus Christ. The Spirit will not abandon us or leave us to our own ways. The decision to seek Him and Him to grow in us, our whole life can change. America can be blessed again.

What are your eyes focusing on today? The day is coming when we can clearly see Him face to face. Sin has blinded many in our nation. "For God did not send the Son into the world to judge the world, but that the world might be saved through Him" (John 3:17 NASU).

For America to see the face of God, we must honor the person of God. We need to worship the King of Kings and the Lord of Lords. "For now we see in a mirror dimly, but then face to face; now I know in part, but then I will know fully just as I also have been fully known." (1 Corinthians 13:12 NASU).

Praising & Praying Across America is all about seeking the heart of Jesus and seeing his face. Jesus is seeking you and your face. In Jesus we see the face of God, see Him looking into our eyes, and hear him saying to us individually and as a nation. "For God did not send Me into the world to judge the world, but that the world might be saved through Me" (John 3:17 NASU).

PRAISING THROUGH THE SILENCE

DR. PHIL WARE

A bright University of Chicago freshman was taking literary classics and rewriting them in 20 or fewer 140-character tweets. He described their writing style this way: "Imagine if Achilles had a Twitter account and an iPhone, and he was telling his story in real time."

I'm thinking about doing that for our prayers. Maybe we would pray more if we saw prayer as something connected to our lives, like the tweets people send out. Except we would constantly be sending them out to God.

That's what Jesus wants—persistent prayer. Luke 18:1 says, "And he told them a parable to the effect that they ought always to pray and not lose heart" (NIV). Problem is we give up on prayer and we lose heart.

It's easy to lose heart, isn't it? This phrase can be translated "to faint, to be utterly spiritless, to be weary, exhausted." Hurricanes. Economic collapse. Health issues. Relational break downs. Jesus understood that life can take its toll on people, even on those who follow him. His prescription is "always to pray and not lose heart."

It's easy to lose heart. And when we do, it's easy to quit praying. We think we need to read another book or attend another seminar on prayer. We think we are doing something wrong, like we tweeted when we should have picked up the phone and called. But those who have been persistent in prayer understand that God's silence is a common experience for all those who practice prayer.

The story Jesus tells is about a woman who gets what she needs from an unjust judge because she constantly pesters him with her requests. The point is clear: if an unjust judge will grant justice, won't God give you what you need even more?

The counsel of Evagrius the Solitary (4th century Christian monk) is good to keep in mind: Do not be distressed if you do not at

93

once receive from God what you ask. He wishes to give you something better—to make you persevere in your prayer. For what is better than to enjoy the love of God and to be in communion with Him?

Those who have faith are the ones who pray through the silence. They are the ones who pray persistently. In their praying, they may not find the answers they think they need. But they will find the One they need. [7]

THE POWERFUL POSTURE OF HUMILITY

LISA CRUMP

"I am God. That is my name.
I don't franchise my glory, don't endorse the no-god idols" (Isaiah
42:8 The Message).

Humility is a place of heart that I describe as an absence of self-motive or promotion. In my decades of life and ministry, I have found humility to be an inward attitude that *has to be pruned again and again*. Even in writing this, I realize my hesitation to confess that, but the Lord knows and it is to Him that I must answer to.

The root of a lack of humility is pride and we know this evil is how our enemy fell from heaven. Please understand humility is very serious spiritual need because pride is totally offensive to our Lord. Our key verse from Isaiah 42 explains why: His glory cannot be shared with any other. The Lord is the source of all things, totally and completely worthy as Revelation 4:11 heralds,

"Worthy are you, our Lord and God, to receive glory and honor and
power, for you created all things, and by your will they existed and
were created" (NASB).

In my ongoing quest and need for humility in prayer and service to the Lord, I have found Him to be lovingly firm. Yet, it was the year of 2006 that the Father gave me experiences to refer back to when I need more pruning from my own pride.

I had been working full time in a large ministry environment for twelve years. When I started there at the lowest level position, the Lord instructed me to work as if I were in higher level, to really commit my work to Him with my best and not less.

Over the years, I found myself watching for promotions, more income and responsibility. November of that year, I was at a prayer conference in Missouri that held an altar call after griping testimonies of the Holy Spirit moving in other nations.

I felt propelled down front where I wept and wept as the Lord impressed me about my motive, which had become making a name for myself rather than making His name known. I was gripped with this truth in my inward attitudes.

Doing well in your work and being promoted is not wrong, but my motive had taken glory from the Lord. It was such a liberating moment with the Lord because He loved me enough to correct me.

Psalm 51 has become a favorite chapter from that year onward. When the Lord nudges me that I am drifting back into self-motives, I recall 2006 and His truths.

"Create in me a clean heart, O God, and renew a right
spirit within me. Cast me not away from your presence,
and take not your Holy Spirit from me. Restore to me the
joy of your salvation, and uphold me with a willing spirit"
(Psalm 51 :10-12 NIV).

How can we have a fruitful relationship with our Creator without genuine humility? It helps me to reflect on such thoughts as basic as the fact that I cannot even take my next breath without God's awareness and willingness. Our heartbeat is an involuntary response. Neither you nor I can make our heart stop beating. It is completely in His control. You can hold your breath, but only for a little while before another involuntary response for air takes over. What an amazing thing to be so dependent on our Creator! Surely the preservation of these key life functions alone should keep us humble as we approach our Lord with utter awe.

Thus, our prayer life, our personal relationship with our God, must begin with the posture, the heart condition of humility. My time with National Day of Prayer Task Force has taught me a simple acronym in both personal and corporate times using the word: PRAY

P for Praise
R for Repentance

A for Asking
Y for Yielding

As Isaiah 42: 8 states, neither His glory or praise is to be shared with anything or anyone else. Starting my prayer time in praise, honors Him as Jesus instructed from Matthew 6:9, "Our Father in heaven, hallowed be your name" (NIV). There is proper order when beginning in praise to Him that puts my heart in alignment with His. Being aware of my need to repent or confess cleans me in preparation before asking Him about needs. We should tarry on praise and pure worship with any confession needed as there comes a release of any self-stuff within us from this posture, which works to remove pride.

To petition or ask is also important to our heavenly Father in our relationship. One of my favorite passages of scripture is Philippians 4:6 "Do not be anxious about anything, but in everything by prayer and petition, with thanksgiving, present your requests to God" (NIV). Personally, I believe His pleasure can be felt when we are grateful before Him. Thankfulness is a part of humility because it recognizes He alone is the Source to whom we are indebted.

Yielding is surrender to Him in every way. Giving ourselves fully and trusting Him yields to His sovereignty over our own understanding. It often involves waiting; which requires a humble and expectant heart as well.

Humility is also found in someone who exercises the truths found in Proverbs 1:7.

"The fear of the LORD is the beginning of knowledge, but fools despise wisdom and instruction" (NIV).

There are many evidences in our nation of those who do not fear or reverence the Lord. Self-motives birthed in pride seem to reign, yet we know this is a cause of the lack of wisdom in our national scene.

A final aspect of humility in prayer is love. If we follow His first commandment as Mark 12: 30 states, "to love the Lord your God with all our heart, and with all our soul and with all your mind and with all your strength" (NIV), we will want to put ourselves aside for the highest place this leads to. From love of Him first, humility must come.

There we realize His motive in loving us first, we receive that love and return it. Real love places the other before self.

Is the Lord teaching you about the high value He places on humility? Are you going through a painful period dying to self so that He can increase? Please don't feel alone. I am of the persuasion that many Christians face this battle on an ongoing basis. I invite you to join me in asking the Lord to examine us regularly so that we do not take any of His glory or praise. Truly there is a blessed power and peace beyond description when we approach Him with a humble soul.

Praising for Jerusalem—A Place for Prayer

Rev. Linda Chandler

As this book title, *Praising & Praying Across America*, calls us forth into and out of our prayer closets, God will have us encounter a place that is decidedly not often on the American people's radar screen, but is at the center of God's heart. It is a place that shares both time and space with the eternal purposes of God. It is a place we are commanded to pray for: "Pray for the peace of Jerusalem" (Psalm 122:6 NASB) not once but constantly and continually: "You who call upon the Lord, give yourselves no rest and give Him no rest till He establishes Jerusalem and makes her the praise of the earth" (Isaiah 62:6-7 NIV). America, you are spiritually and literally embedded in God's divine purposes that emanated from the city of Jerusalem, do you not see us hidden in there? Let's reveal God's purposes for Jerusalem being our responsibility in our prayer closets.

In the ancient world of the Bible Jerusalem was considered the center of the earth. She is mentioned in the Bible, 881 times, more than any other place. Today she is a city where east meets west and has been called the "epicenter" of the world by the renowned and contemporary author, Joel Rosenberg. As a world constantly in turmoil, Jerusalem is front and center in God's epic story of love and justice. God's story seems to shout from the Heavenly gates: As Jerusalem goes so goes the world! God sends this word through the Prophet Zechariah: "I am going to make Jerusalem a cup that sends all the surrounding peoples reeling" (Zechariah 12:1 NIV). God's measure for "this cup" was given to Abraham, Father of the Jews: "I will bless those who bless you, and whoever curses you I will curse; and all peoples on earth will be blessed through you."

Jerusalem is first recognized by Abraham in God's story of Abraham meeting with Melechizedek, King of Salem. Salem means *"peace"* and was the ancient site of Jerusalem (Genesis 14:18-20). King

Melechizedek blessed Abraham and Abraham returned the blessing on the king and city of Salem by giving a tenth of all he owned. Jeremiah prophesies a day when the LORD will fully restore Israel and Jerusalem will be called "The throne of the LORD, and all nations will gather in Jerusalem to honor the name of the Lord" (Jeremiah 3:17 NIV). Finally, in the last days, Jerusalem will become "the city of the great King" (Matthew 5:35 NIV) and will take her curtain call as "the bride, the wife of the Lamb…the Holy City, Jerusalem, coming down out of heaven from God…(shining) with the glory of God" (Revelation 21:9-11 NIV).

For us who call ourselves Christian, Jerusalem stands both as a witness to the purposes of the Divine, and as an echo of the Bride with whom Messiah Jesus began the birthing process of new sons and daughters for the Kingdom through resurrection. These sons and daughters are the spiritual inheritance guaranteed to the Son in Psalm 2:7-8 "I will proclaim the Lord's decree: He said to me, 'You are my son; today I become your father. Ask me, and I will make the nations your inheritance; the ends of the earth your possession'" (NIV). As those who follow the Way of Jesus the Messiah, Jerusalem becomes our place of birthing. On that day of Passover, long ago, as the sword pierced the side of our crucified savior, blood and water gushed forth and joined with the ground of Jerusalem, symbolically producing new birth and new beginnings. It is a reminder of the distant past in The Garden when God reached into man's side and drew forth woman. This day of "piercing the side" would produce and call forth the nations from the sacred ground of Jerusalem. No longer would only the Jews carry God's story but the whole world would now be grafted in through the Jewish Son of God, Jesus, who reminds us in Revelation. "I am the Root and the offspring of David…" (Revelation 22:16 NIV)

Now, Jerusalem, the city of kings and the Jewish capital of Israel, becomes as our birth mother. Our spiritual umbilical cord has come forth from the Jewish root and Jewish ground and the vine of God's purposes will emerge to encapsulate the world! It is no wonder that God would call us forth to honor Jerusalem with our prayers. "Honor your father and your mother, as the Lord your God has commanded you, so that you may live long and that it may go well with you in the land the Lord your God is giving you" (Deuteronomy 5:16 NIV). Prayers of honor and praise for our birthplace and spiritual mother,

Jerusalem, bring forth blessings of life and wellness. Next, we continue in our prayers for Jerusalem by focusing on Psalm 122:2-5.

> "Our feet are standing
> In your gates, O Jerusalem.
> Jerusalem is built like a city
> that is closely compacted together
> That is where the tribes go up,
> the tribes of the Lord
> To praise the name of the Lord
> according to the statute given to Israel.
> There the thrones for judgment stand,
> the thrones of the house of David" (NIV).

We like the tribes of old should offer prayer which "praise the Name of the Lord." Praise God for what He has done, what He is now doing and what He will do in the not too distant future for and with Jerusalem. Pray for our Nation of America to be a blessing and not a cursed obstacle when God uses Jerusalem as His cup of measure. Believe and trust these prayers to resound and echo throughout the courts of heaven; for we are praying for Jerusalem to fully realize her destiny as the City of the Great King and the city where the thrones of judgment stand.

Finally pray as God commands: "… for the peace of Jerusalem" so she will fulfill her destiny as God's City of Peace. Our prayers for peace should pull from a definition of peace. Pray for peace evidenced in calm; tranquility among the inhabitants, harmony in the homes, and for Jerusalem to be a location that imbues quiet, stillness, reconciliation and tranquility. These prayers become our witness that we desire for God's will to be done and for Jerusalem to be established as "praise in all the earth"!

Praying in Obedience

Carole Lewis

"Love the Lord your God with all your heart and with all
your soul and with all your mind and with all your strength"
(Mark 12:30 NIV).

Jesus, when asked what is the greatest commandment, gave the statement above. The single greatest truth I have learned through many years of ministry is that God's love language is obedience. Jesus said, "If you love me, you will obey me" (John 14:21-24 NIV).

I directed First Place 4 Health for more than 30 years and the core of this program is learning to give Christ first place in every area of life; emotional, spiritual, mental, and physical. As we learn to love God with our whole person, our life comes into balance and God can use us greatly.

Love God With All Your Heart

I have learned that my emotions cannot be trusted. The Bible has much to say about my heart.

- Man looks on the outside, but God looks at the heart.
  (1 Samuel 16:7)
- The heart is deceitful above all things; who can know it?.
  (Jeremiah 17:9
- Out of the overflow of the heart, the mouth speaks.
  (Luke 6:45)

I go to a water aerobics class every Saturday. Last week I woke up and didn't want to go. I wasn't sick and had no other appointments, I just didn't want to get up and go. After going back and forth for a while in my mind, will, and emotions, I took some of my own advice to "Do the next right thing," put on my suit and went to the pool.

Zig Ziglar said, "It is easier to act your way into a new way of feeling than it is to feel your way into a new way of acting." When I do the next right thing, I am saying to my emotions, "You're not the boss of me." Learning to love God with my heart means that my emotions will follow my actions, not the other way around.

Love God With All Your Soul

I have learned that God desires a relationship with me that is up close and personal. My dear friends know they will hear from me on a regular basis by phone. I want to hear their voice so I call my friends when I go outside to walk. My Father in heaven wants to hear my voice too and longs for me to come to Him early and often. I have a cat named Lacey. When I got Lacey a few months ago, she was 2 years old and well behaved. She slept on the end of the bed. She ate a spoonful of wet food morning and night along with her dry food. Now that I have established a relationship with Lacey, things have changed. She sleeps in the crook of my arm, and if I turn over in the night, she moves to the other side. She now eats an entire 5 ounces can of wet food a day in addition to her dry food. She tries to sit in my lap when I am having my quiet time to the point that I have to go to the table to be alone. Even then, she jumps up on the chair to be next to me. Lacey is teaching me that God desires the same kind of relationship with me. He never gets tired of hearing me or seeing me because He loves me, and I am His child. How do I get better at reading my Bible, studying my Bible, and praying? By spending time every day with Jesus, the lover of my soul.

Loving God With All Your Mind

Our minds are high functioning computers. Every thought, feeling and action by us or others is stored in our minds. The way we think has a direct effect on the way we act and many of us have a lot of faulty thinking. Romans 12:2 tells us, "Do not conform any longer to the pattern of this world, but be transformed by the renewing of your mind. Then you will be able to test and approve what God's will is – His good, pleasing and perfect will"(NIV). Scripture memory is a vital part of the First Place 4 Health program, and I have been able to learn more than100 verses over the years. These verses are stored deep in my mind and heart. In 2001 on Thanksgiving night, our daughter, Shari, was killed by a drunk driver. Shari left behind her husband and three daughters, 19, 15 and 13. It was the Scripture I had memorized that saved my life. I remember many nights waking up in the middle of the night having, what I can only describe as "Mama thoughts." Who will be there for the girls' weddings? Who will be there for the birth of their babies? As I lay in bed thinking these thoughts, I would realize that a Scripture verse was in my mind, and it was always a verse I had memorized. The truth of the Word of God is what will change us, and it will change us from the inside out. The only way I have seen people learn to think right is knowing Scripture and learning how to apply it when life is messy.

LOVING GOD WITH ALL YOUR STRENGTH

This body is the only one you and I are going to get. I have learned that my body doesn't want to do "The next right thing." In fact, my body desires to do those things that will tear it down. My friend, Jennifer Kennedy Dean, wrote a book, *Altar'd*. In that book, she says that God's desire is for us to lay these bodies on the altar; give our flesh to Him. She says that "our flesh makes promises it cannot keep." "Film, flam, flesh," she calls it. It has taken me more than 30 years, but I am learning that if I take good care of this body, it will serve me well. If I eat healthy foods, walk, ride my bike, or do strength training several times a week, my body will respond in a positive way. I do not take good health for granted, and I'm thrilled not to be taking any medicine or have any physical problems in my 70s. Studies have proven that 80% of all cancers could be avoided if we eat right and exercise.

Prayer and obedience go hand in hand. Pray and obey; it's the only way.

Praying for Godly Leaders

Dr. Kie Bowman

America suffers from a political leadership shortage. As usual, there are still plenty of people vying for power, positions, and privilege but the leadership we all want and need must offer far more than personal advantage to the person who wins the race. Leaders who deserve to win our support must ultimately be leaders who help us, the American people - not merely be clever but unprincipled tacticians who have discovered the easiest ways to help themselves. Where do we find the leaders we need?

As I write this article we are still weeks away from the 2016 Presidential election, and while both major candidates have strong and passionate followings, their most ardent supporters are on the fringes. The larger electorate must settle on the lesser of two evils, (if they vote at all for one of the major party candidates). To demonstrate my point, consider the most recent Gallup Poll which finds the majority of Americans have an unfavorable view of both leading candidates- one of whom has already been elected by the time you read this. In other words, we are electing, by majority, a leader the majority of people don't want and don't like. We suffer from a leadership vacuum.

What causes this conundrum? Are there really so few people prepared for political leadership? Is the process flawed so the best people cannot reach the top? Or, are we so hopelessly polarized politically we can only expect candidates who arrive at the finish line fatally bloodied up by the process? Does the common practice of using sophisticated opposition research, the scandalously negative campaigning, and the endless electronic trail of past statements and positions, leave us stuck with leaders who are so diminished in our eyes by the time they reach office we find it almost impossible to support them or trust the institutions they represent? Or is the problem something else? Is the problem less the process and more about the people who choose to run?

These provocative questions need not remain unanswered or ignored. They should nag at our conscience, and almost unavoidably guide our thinking toward different conclusions for some future battle. Since we are capable of learning from our past, what are the lessons we take from an election driven by reality show vulgarity, and WikiLeaks exposes? The presidential race of 2016 has not been our finest hour, but it's never too soon to start improving, since someday it may be too late.

Great leaders still exist. I see them every day. On the whole, I believe our best leaders are leading our churches. Pastors and church leaders today are incredible. In the United States, they are leading some of the largest and most effective churches in the history of Christianity. The surprising thing about these pastors is not the fact they are great leaders. Western civilization since the time of Christ has been shaped by the courage and convictions of church leaders. From Martin Luther to Martin Luther King, the church has perennially offered us some of our most exceptional leaders. The most curious fact about today's generation of church leaders is the context in which they lead- and it is here we find a ray of light shining out from the grey skies of political leadership.

These exceptional pastors lead growing churches in a culture which is trending away from church attendance and historically held views about Christianity itself. Yet, in spite of these accelerating changes in culture, more and more often today, remarkable churches led by gifted pastors continue to defy the unmistakable trends of secularism, skepticism, and blatant militant atheism so common in 21st century America. In fact, the most gifted leaders and the largest, fastest growing, and most influential churches in America have grown and flourished in a culture increasingly unfriendly to the church and the biblical Christian message. How?

It's counter intuitive when churches grow faster and larger against a secular backdrop but Scripture reminds us, "Where sin increased, grace abounded all the more" (Romans 5:20 ESV). In other words, these talented leaders, relying upon timeless principles of leadership, are leading growing churches in spite of, rather than because of their often hostile cultural context.

By now I can almost hear you thinking, "So what? How does the growth of the mega church in an anti-church culture help us find better political leaders?" That's a good question.

While there are always a few disappointing examples of leaders who "flame out" and embarrass themselves and their cause, the vast majority of Christian leaders, when viewed collectively, are still among the most influential voices in our culture at the moment. That's true, if for no other reason, because through their numerous ministries, available today on a wide variety of platforms (and networked like internet cable into every corner of the United States), these leaders routinely influence the thinking and lives of millions of Americans. In other words, the lesson for politics, learned from the tenacious proliferation of America's persistently determined churches is clear-people still follow better leaders with good ideas. And lesson two, while counter cultural on its face, is nevertheless true-the best leaders in the country are those who are driven by a clear sense of Christian mission.

Assuming for a moment these observations have merit, what are the practical implications? How can a broken political system, existing to the satisfaction of almost no one, ever be improved by the most naturally organic leadership rich movement in America-the church? Actually, it's not that complicated.

Obviously, for many years, a few well known, high-profile pastors, as well as a virtual militia of local pastors in smaller congregations, have been organized to support causes important to "values voters." We should assume, based on the current level of rhetoric and the most recent past election cycles, nationally known and influential Christian leaders, as well grass roots level pastors, will continue to be a factor in future elections. Like almost everything else in the election cycle of 2016, however, the conventional wisdom about Christian unity around a political party was unexpectedly pre-empted by the unconventional juggernaut of the Trump candidacy. Pastors and Christian leaders were more divided in the General Election this time around. Of course, it is impossible to predict with accuracy how those passionately argued divisions will affect potential unity in future election cycles. But when considered from the larger perspective of what matters most to Christian leaders, there is virtually no reason to view the currently fractured band of brothers as being a group divided along politically ideological lines. Instead, they just ardently disagreed about the candidate himself. With that having been said, if given the opportunity to galvanize around a different person, who more closely represents their political and moral positions, Christian leaders should be expected to rally solidly behind future candidates who champion the mostly predictable causes that drive Christians to the polls. At the risk of over simplifying the debate, the future of Christian political unity will come down to better leaders running for office.

Beyond the personal involvement of Christian leaders, however, the issue of leadership is a consequential factor with implications that reach deeper into the American populace, and affect far more people than just the top tier of America's mega church pastors. Every informed voter recognizes we have a national shortage of political leadership. While it is also true there are some qualified, gifted, and exceptional individuals who will run and who currently hold office, it is equally obvious the pool of principled leaders who can mount a national campaign, and garner the support needed to lead a majority in a pluralistic culture, is getting shallower every year.

As America's demographic and social map continues to rapidly change, and voters become more polarized and hardened in their individual political philosophies and preferences, quality leadership is both more needed and harder to find than ever before.

Therefore, given these challenges, a handful of potential solutions seem self-evident. For one thing, younger citizens must get involved, not merely in campaigning for other candidates, but by running for office themselves. Men and women who have learned leadership in the context of America's faith communities, and have had that leadership tested in businesses, courtroom experience, and public service must deepen the pool of candidates for future elections. In a word, we need more, younger and more ethnically diverse leaders involved in the political process.

People of faith must encourage their children and grandchildren, as well as the students in their churches, to pursue higher education in government and law, as well as business and leadership. In that way, the best can be identified and encouraged to pursue leadership in the public sector.

Going forward we must also insist upon a definition of leadership, regardless of the age or gender of the leader, which involves more than gaining power. Leadership is based instead on the quality of ideas for the common good, and the personal ethics of the leaders themselves. In an age of widespread changes in what the culture deems morally acceptable, personal sexual ethics and the virtues of honesty and integrity will still attract the most supporters from a voting public weary from the failures of people who want to lead us.

Finally, for those concerned citizens who are disheartened by the undisguised ugliness of the current political process, leadership is required from them too. Everyone concerned with the future of the nation must stay involved and support the candidates and the ideas they believe in. It should go without saying, leaders in a democracy vote! After all, in America we still effect change one vote at a time.

We learned again in 2016 the importance of personal choices in the private as well as the public lives of our aspiring leaders, and how those issues still matter deeply to the American people. As a result, leaders in the political arena must be people with virtues and lifestyles, which we find most frequently fashioned in the houses of worship throughout our country. Good leaders can sway voters who disagree about policy, but it is much more difficult to convince good people a bad person will make a good leader. Character still counts in our political leaders.

Great leaders are still among us, even though it may be harder than ever to coax them into politics, given the brutal process of running a successful campaign. If good people refuse to serve, however, the choices we are left with will only get worse.

If ever there was a time for leaders to lead, now is the time. The old adage is still true, "Everything rises and falls on leadership." For me, and I suspect for millions of others, it's time to see more rising and less falling in the lives of those who propose to lead us. America deserves, and desperately needs our very best out front and in the lead. It is likely we will find the most capable future leaders emerging from America's most reliable home grown leadership matrix- our churches.

Praising in the Pits

Rev. Brian Alarid

Through Jesus, therefore, let us continually offer to God a sacrifice of
praise—the fruit of lips that openly profess his name
(Hebrews 13:15 NIV).

Make a wish," we said. She closed her eyes, took a deep breath,
and blew out her birthday candles. Chloe, our oldest daughter,
had just turned twelve and an exciting year awaited her. She was the
happiest we had ever seen her. Her grades were spectacular. She had
excelled at basketball and was now running track in the hopes of
becoming a quicker and stronger athlete. At church, she sang on the
worship team and loved every minute of it. Life was really good.

Then, out of the blue, Chloe got sick. At first, we thought she
was just tired from all the track meets and late nights doing homework.
One day, two days, three days went by and Chloe was not improving.
By the fourth day, her stomach pain was so intense we had to rush her
to the emergency room. That was the first of her many hospital stays
to date. Doctors and specialists in several hospitals were baffled by her
case and could not give us an accurate diagnosis for the cause of her
pain.

With no real answers after months of tests, medications that do
not work, and debilitating pain, Chloe spends most of her days in bed.
She is too weak to do what she loves, too sensitive to light and noise to
spend time with friends and family.

Believe me, there is nothing more excruciating than seeing pain
and hurt in your child's eyes and not having the power to fix it. We
have prayed, fasted and pleaded with God to heal her, but four months
later, Chloe is still sick and our hearts are still broken. If you ask me,
this is the *pits*! I wish this chapter was a glowing testimony of healing
that you could take comfort in, but instead, I am taking a page from

one of the most difficult chapters in our lives and sharing it with you as it unfolds.

Even though God has not healed Chloe yet, He has answered our prayers. Perhaps not in the way we wanted or expected, but He has answered them. He's told us time and time again, "Your breakthrough is in your praise." We believe these six simple words hold the key to our miracle and, who knows, maybe yours too. Anybody can praise when they are getting blessed. Anybody can praise God when they get a promotion, a raise, a new house, a better job and a boost to their health. But will you praise God in the pits?

The Apostle Paul was no stranger to pits. 2 Corinthians 11:23-29 vividly describes some of the pits he had found himself in while doing God's will: floggings, shipwrecks, danger, sleepless nights, hunger, thirst, beatings, and yes, even prison. Acts 16:25 describes one of Paul's nights inside a prison cell. Paul and Silas had already been stripped, beaten with rods and flogged for casting out a demon from a fortune-teller. But it is their attitude of praise, and not their suffering, that takes center stage in verse 26.

> "About midnight Paul and Silas were praying and singing hymns to
> God, and the other prisoners were listening to them" (NIV).

How did Paul and Silas respond to this unfair treatment and imprisonment? Did they get mad at God and say, "I can't believe this! Here we are preaching your Word and we end up beaten and arrested under your watch. What's wrong with you God?" Did they get mad at the people who beat them or spend the night plotting their revenge? Not Paul. Not Silas.

What did they choose to do? Their response to adversity was to pray and sing praises to God. Say what? They did not waste a single second on complaints, self-pity, or revenge. Instead, Paul and Silas turned pain into heartfelt prayer and sadness into joyful singing. And what happened when they sang and prayed is the stuff of legends:

> "Suddenly there was such a violent earthquake that the foundations
> of the prison were shaken. At once all the prison doors flew open,
> and everyone's chains came loose" (Acts 16:26, NLT).

Their breakthrough was in their praise. And I might add, that their chains were not the only ones that came off that night. Every single prisoner saw chains fall off their hands and feet too. When we pray and praise in the pits of life, God sends breakthrough, and it doesn't just impact us—it brings freedom to those around us as well. What if your breakthrough is the key to answered prayers for your family, your church and your community? If you pray and praise God in the midst of your difficult circumstances, God's response will astound you.

You might be down right now. But God is with you and the only way out of that pit is to begin praising God with everything that's inside of you. Praise God out of your financial lack, out of your loneliness, out of your pain, out of your sickness, out of your addiction, out of your failure, out of your depression.

David said in Psalm 23:4, "Yea though I walk through the valley of the shadow of death, I will fear no evil for Thou art with me" (KJV). Pay close attention to David's words. He said he was walking *through* the valley of the shadow of death. That means he didn't plan on staying there. This valley was temporary, not permanent.

Winston Churchill once said, "If you are going through hell… don't stop." In other words, keep on walking until you get to safety. Hebrews 13:15 tells us to "continually offer to God a sacrifice of praise—the fruit of lips that openly profess his name" (NIV). No trial or difficulty has the power in itself to stop your praise or your prayers from ascending to heaven's throne.

In my case, I can't make Chloe better. I haven't been able to find that one medication that takes away her pain. But there are two things I can do. In fact, there are two things I will do—I will *pray* and I will *praise*. Every time she wakes up in pain in the middle of the night, my wife and I push anxiety aside and we pray. When blood tests come back to remind us of incurable health challenges, we choose to give God our sacrifice of praise. We recall God's goodness to us in the past and we celebrate his future mercies.

I can honestly say that we are living out Paul and Silas' experience in our own prison cell of sorts. We are bruised and broken by this sickness, and some days it feels like the very foundation of our lives is being shaken. At the same time, we firmly believe that one day Chloe will resume a normal life. She will play basketball again. The sound of her friends giggling and talking will once again fill our home.

We will see her worship God at our church and on many stages around the world.

But in the meantime, we will continue to praise the One who alone can break chains and open prison doors. When we climb out of this pit, Chloe will be healed and we will be chain-free—free of worry, fear and unbelief. And so will you and your loved ones. Your breakthrough is on the way, so just keep praising Jesus until it becomes a reality.

Never forget this one simple, powerful truth—your breakthrough is in your praise. This is as true for us as it is for our nation. America is in the pits right now. Politically, our nation is the most divided it has been in my lifetime. People have lost faith in our government. The economy is hanging on by a thread. Our national debt is out of control. Racial tensions are the highest they have been since the 60s. Police officers go to work with great trepidation, knowing they might become a target simply because of their uniform. Our educational system is broken. Americans are angry and disillusioned. Our only hope is Jesus Christ. And the only way out of this pit is for God's people all across America to pray and praise the Lord.

A turnaround seems impossible, but like Jesus said in Matthew 19:26, "With man this is impossible, but with God all things are possible" (NIV). Prayer and praise have the power to elevate us out of the realm of the impossible into the realm where anything is possible. Don't give up. Be of good cheer. God is listening to your prayers and reveling in your praise. Our breakthrough is right around the corner as we praise and pray.

UNIT 8
DAILY PRAISE & PRAYER JOURNAL

7 X 7 X 7 PLAN

Adopt a Leader

49 Days of Prayer Daily Journal

7 x 7 x 7 Plan

The *Praising & Praying Across America* plan is 7 minutes per day for 7 days a week for 7 weeks. This 7 x7 x 7 plan covers the next 49 days.

For each day for the next 49 days,

✝ Read the verse for the day.

✝ Identify a need, praise, or current news event that will be your prayer focus for the day.

✝ Record that focus on the daily page.

✝ Pray for the elected officials listed and then pray for the leader that you choose in the Adopt a Leader section.

✝ Each day pray for our national culture using the Freedom Seven on page 44 asking the Lord to direct our leaders and lead the people of our nation.

✝ As you continue to pray for America, remember to write a note of encouragement to one of our nation's leaders.

ADOPT A LEADER

Ask God to give you a special desire to pray for one leader specifically.

Write the name and information about that person in the space below.

You will be prompted to pray for that person each day during your 49 days of Praise & Prayer.

Name_____

Position _____

Birthday _____

Spouse _____

Former Positions _____

Children _____

You may write to your legislators at the following addresses:

The Honorable (insert name of Senator)

The Honorable (insert name of Representative)

Each representative and senator has a different address. You may find the best information about how to connect with each one, addressing issues or asking for help at https://www.senate.gov/senators/contact/

49 Days
Praise & Prayer
Journal

Day 1—Date _____
LOVING HIS WORD: WISDOM

Ephesians 1:15-19a (The Message)

That's why, when I heard of the solid trust you have in the Master Jesus and your outpouring of love to all the followers of Jesus, I couldn't stop thanking God for you—every time I prayed, I'd think of you and give thanks. But I do more than thank. I ask—ask the God of our Master, Jesus Christ, to make you intelligent and discerning in knowing him personally, your eyes focused and clear, so that you can see exactly what it is he is calling you to do.

PRAISING & PRAYING HIS WORD

Specific Need or Event: _____

Praise & Prayer for President Donald Trump

_____

_____

Praise & Prayer for Vice President Mike Pence

_____

_____

Praise & Prayer for Secretary of State Rex Tillerson

_____

_____

Praise & Prayer for Attorney General Jeff Sessions

_____

_____

Praise & Prayer for My Adopted Leader

_____

_____

Praise & Prayer for Today's FREEDOM SEVEN (See Chapter 11.)
Praise & Prayer for My Family

Day 2—Date _____
LOVING HIS WORD: PERSONAL SAFETY

Proverbs 18:4-10 (The Message)

Many words rush along like rivers in flood, but deep wisdom flows up from artesian springs. It's not right to go easy on the guilty, or come down hard on the innocent. The words of a fool start fights; do him a favor and gag him. Fools are undone by their big mouths; their souls are crushed by their words. Slack habits and sloppy work are as bad as vandalism God's name is a place of protection— good people can run there and be safe.

PRAISING & PRAYING HIS WORD

Specific Need or Event: _____

Praise & Prayer for President Donald Trump

_____

_____

Praise & Prayer for Vice President Mike Pence

_____

_____

Praise & Prayer for Secretary of State Rex Tillerson

_____

_____

Praise & Prayer for Attorney General Jeff Sessions

_____

_____

Praise & Prayer for My Adopted Leader

_____

_____

Praise & Prayer for Today's FREEDOM SEVEN (See Chapter 11.)

Praise & Prayer for My Family

DAY 3—DATE _____
LOVING HIS WORD: REJOICE & PRAY ALWAYS

1 THESSALONIANS 5:12-17 (NCSB)

Now we ask you, brothers, to give recognition to those who labor among you and lead you in the Lord and admonish you, and to regard them very highly in love because of their work. Be at peace among yourselves. And we exhort you, brothers: warn those who are irresponsible, comfort the discouraged, help the weak, be patient with everyone. ...but always pursue what is good for one another and for all. Rejoice always! Pray constantly.

PRAISING & PRAYING HIS WORD

Specific Need or Event: _____

Praise & Prayer for President Donald Trump

_____

_____

Praise & Prayer for Vice President Mike Pence

_____

_____

Praise & Prayer for Secretary of State Rex Tillerson

_____

_____

Praise & Prayer for Attorney General Jeff Sessions

_____

_____

Praise & Prayer for My Adopted Leader

_____

_____

Praise & Prayer for Today's FREEDOM SEVEN (See Chapter 11.)

Praise & Prayer for My Family

DAY 4—DATE _____
LOVING HIS WORD: GRACE UNDER PRESSURE

PSALM 5:1-3 (THE MESSAGE)

Listen, GOD! Please, pay attention!
Can you make sense of these ramblings, my groans and cries? King-God, I need your help.
Every morning you'll hear me at it again.
Every morning I lay out the pieces of my life on your altar and watch for fire to descend.

PRAISING & PRAYING HIS WORD

Specific Need or Event: _____

Praise & Prayer for President Donald Trump

_____

_____

Praise & Prayer for Vice President Mike Pence

_____

_____

Praise & Prayer for Secretary of State Rex Tillerson

_____

_____

Praise & Prayer for Attorney General Jeff Sessions

_____

_____

Praise & Prayer for My Adopted Leader

_____

_____

Praise & Prayer for Today's FREEDOM SEVEN (See Chapter 11.)
Praise & Prayer for My Family

DAY 5—DATE _____
LOVING HIS WORD: PRAISE WITH PEACE

PHILIPPIANS 4:6-7 (THE MESSAGE)

Don't fret or worry. Instead of worrying, pray. Let petitions and praises shape your worries into prayers, letting God know your concerns. Before you know it, a sense of God's wholeness, everything coming together for good, will come and settle you down. It's wonderful what happens when Christ displaces worry at the center of your life.

PRAISING & PRAYING HIS WORD

Specific Need or Event: _____

Praise & Prayer for President Donald Trump

_____

_____

Praise & Prayer for Vice President Mike Pence

_____

_____

Praise & Prayer for Secretary of State Rex Tillerson

_____

_____

Praise & Prayer for Attorney General Jeff Sessions

_____

_____

Praise & Prayer for My Adopted Leader

_____

_____

Praise & Prayer for Today's FREEDOM SEVEN (See Chapter 11.)

Praise & Prayer for My Family

DAY 6—DATE _____
LOVING HIS WORD: STRENGTH WITHOUT DOUBT

MATTHEW 21:21-22 (THE MESSAGE)

But Jesus was matter-of-fact: "Yes—and if you embrace this kingdom life and don't doubt God, you'll not only do minor feats like I did to the fig tree, but also triumph over huge obstacles.

PRAISING & PRAYING HIS WORD

Specific Need or Event: _____

Praise & Prayer for President Donald Trump

_____

_____

Praise & Prayer for Vice President Mike Pence

_____

_____

Praise & Prayer for Secretary of State Rex Tillerson

_____

_____

Praise & Prayer for Attorney General Jeff Sessions

_____

_____

Praise & Prayer for My Adopted Leader

_____

_____

Praise & Prayer for Today's FREEDOM SEVEN (See Chapter 11.)

Praise & Prayer for My Family

DAY 7—DATE _____
LOVING HIS WORD: Mountainous Moments

MATTHEW 21:21-22 (THE MESSAGE)
This mountain, for instance, you'll tell, 'Go jump in the lake,' and it will jump. Absolutely everything, ranging from small to large, as you make it a part of your believing prayer, gets included as you lay hold of God."

PRAISING & PRAYING HIS WORD

Specific Need or Event: _____

Praise & Prayer for President Donald Trump

_____

_____

Praise & Prayer for Vice President Mike Pence

_____

_____

Praise & Prayer for Secretary of State Rex Tillerson

_____

_____

Praise & Prayer for Attorney General Jeff Sessions

_____

_____

Praise & Prayer for My Adopted Leader

_____

_____

Praise & Prayer for Today's FREEDOM SEVEN (See Chapter 11.)

Praise & Prayer for My Family

DAY 8—DATE _____
LOVING HIS WORD: Extravagant Love

Ephesians 3:15-19 (The Message)

My response is to get down on my knees before the Father, this magnificent Father who parcels out all heaven and earth. I ask him to strengthen you by his Spirit—not a brute strength but a glorious inner strength—that Christ will live in you as you open the door and invite him in. And I ask him that with both feet planted firmly on love, you'll be able to take in with all followers of Jesus the extravagant dimensions of Christ's love. Reach out and experience the breadth! Test its length! Plumb the depths! Rise to the heights! Live…full in the fullness of God.

PRAISING & PRAYING HIS WORD

Specific Need or Event: _____

Praise & Prayer for President Donald Trump

_____

_____

Praise & Prayer for Vice President Mike Pence

_____

_____

Praise & Prayer for Secretary of State Rex Tillerson

_____

_____

Praise & Prayer for Attorney General Jeff Sessions

_____

_____

Praise & Prayer for My Adopted Leader

_____

_____

Praise & Prayer for Today's FREEDOM SEVEN (See Chapter 11.)
Praise & Prayer for My Family

DAY 9—DATE _____
LOVING HIS WORD: ABUNDANT JOY

PSALM 67:1-7 (THE MESSAGE)

God, mark us with grace and blessing! Smile! The whole country will see how you work, all the godless nations see how you save. God! Let people thank and enjoy you. Let all people thank and enjoy you. Let all far-flung people become happy and shout their happiness because you judge them fair and square, you tend the far-flung peoples. God! Let people thank and enjoy you. Let all people thank and enjoy you. Earth, display your exuberance! You mark us with blessing, O God, our God. You mark us with blessing, O God. Earth's four corners—honor him!

PRAISING & PRAYING HIS WORD

Specific Need or Event: _____

Praise & Prayer for President Donald Trump

_____

_____

Praise & Prayer for Vice President Mike Pence

_____

_____

Praise & Prayer for Secretary of State Rex Tillerson

_____

_____

Praise & Prayer for Attorney General Jeff Sessions

_____

_____

Praise & Prayer for My Adopted Leader

_____

_____

Praise & Prayer for Today's FREEDOM SEVEN (See Chapter 11.)
Praise & Prayer for My Family

DAY 10—DATE _____
LOVING HIS WORD: PURPOSE WITH GOD

COLOSSIANS 1:15-18 (THE MESSAGE)

We look at this Son and see the God who cannot be seen. We look at this Son and see God's original purpose in everything created. For everything, absolutely everything, above and below, visible and invisible, rank after rank after rank of angels—*everything* got started in him and finds its purpose in him. He was there before any of it came into existence and holds it all together right up to this moment

PRAISING & PRAYING HIS WORD

Specific Need or Event: _____

Praise & Prayer for President Donald Trump

_____

_____

Praise & Prayer for Vice President Mike Pence

_____

_____

Praise & Prayer for Secretary of State Rex Tillerson

_____

_____

Praise & Prayer for Attorney General Jeff Sessions

_____

_____

Praise & Prayer for My Adopted Leader

_____

_____

Praise & Prayer for Today's FREEDOM SEVEN (See Chapter 11.)

Praise & Prayer for My Family

DAY 11—DATE _____
LOVING HIS WORD: PATIENCE IN TRIAL

EPHESIANS 6:13-18 (THE MESSAGE)

Be prepared. You're up against far more than you can handle on your own. Take all the help you can get, every weapon God has issued, so that when it's all over but the shouting you'll still be on your feet. Truth, righteousness, peace, faith, and salvation are more than words. Learn how to apply them. You'll need them throughout your life. God's Word is an *indispensable* weapon. In the same way, prayer is essential in this ongoing warfare. Pray hard and long. Pray for your brothers and sisters. Keep your eyes open. Keep each other's spirits up so that no one falls behind or drops out.

PRAISING & PRAYING HIS WORD

Specific Need or Event: _____

Praise & Prayer for President Donald Trump

_____

_____

Praise & Prayer for Vice President Mike Pence

_____

_____

Praise & Prayer for Secretary of State Rex Tillerson

_____

_____

Praise & Prayer for Attorney General Jeff Sessions

_____

_____

Praise & Prayer for My Adopted Leader

_____

_____

Praise & Prayer for Today's FREEDOM SEVEN (See Chapter 11.)
Praise & Prayer for My Family

DAY 12—DATE _____
LOVING HIS WORD: PRAYERFUL INFLUENCE

JEREMIAH 33:2-8 (THE MESSAGE)

This is God's Message, the God who made earth, made it livable and lasting... "Call to me and I will answer you. I'll tell you marvelous and wondrous things that you could never figure out on your own." This is what God, the God of Israel, has to say about what's going on in this city, about the homes of both people and kings that have been demolished, about all the ravages of war and the killing... "But now take another look. I'm going to give this city a thorough renovation, working a true healing inside and out. I'm going to show them life whole, life brimming with blessings.

PRAISING & PRAYING HIS WORD

Specific Need or Event: _____

Praise & Prayer for President Donald Trump

_____

_____

Praise & Prayer for Vice President Mike Pence

_____

_____

Praise & Prayer for Secretary of State Rex Tillerson

_____

_____

Praise & Prayer for Attorney General Jeff Sessions

_____

_____

Praise & Prayer for My Adopted Leader

_____

_____

Praise & Prayer for Today's FREEDOM SEVEN (See Chapter 11.)
Praise & Prayer for My Family

DAY 13—DATE _____
LOVING HIS WORD: LOVE OF LIBERTY

JAMES 1:24-25 (THE MESSAGE)

Don't fool yourself into thinking that you are a listener when you are anything but, letting the Word go in one ear and out the other. Act on what you hear! Those who hear and don't act are like those who glance in the mirror, walk away, and two minutes later have no idea who they are, what they look like. But whoever catches a glimpse of the revealed counsel of God—the free life!—even out of the corner of his eye, and sticks with it, is no distracted scatterbrain but a man or woman of action. That person will find delight and affirmation in the action.

PRAISING & PRAYING HIS WORD

Specific Need or Event: _____

Praise & Prayer for President Donald Trump

_____

_____

Praise & Prayer for Vice President Mike Pence

_____

_____

Praise & Prayer for Secretary of State Rex Tillerson

_____

_____

Praise & Prayer for Attorney General Jeff Sessions

_____

_____

Praise & Prayer for My Adopted Leader

_____

_____

Praise & Prayer for Today's FREEDOM SEVEN (See Chapter 11.)
Praise & Prayer for My Family

DAY 14—DATE _____
LOVING HIS WORD: FAITH AND ENDURANCE

2 THESSALONIANS 3:3-9 (THE MESSAGE)

Pray for us. Pray that the Master's Word will simply take off and race through the country to a groundswell of response, just as it did among you…. May the Master take you by the hand and lead you along the path of God's love and Christ's endurance. Our orders—backed up by the Master, Jesus—are to refuse to have anything to do with those among you who are lazy and refuse to work the way we taught you. Don't permit them to freeload on the rest. We showed you how to pull your weight when we were with you, so get on with it. …We simply wanted to provide an example of diligence, hoping it would prove contagious.

PRAISING & PRAYING HIS WORD

Specific Need or Event: _____

Praise & Prayer for President Donald Trump

_____

_____

Praise & Prayer for Vice President Mike Pence

_____

_____

Praise & Prayer for Secretary of State Rex Tillerson

_____

_____

Praise & Prayer for Attorney General Jeff Sessions

_____

_____

Praise & Prayer for My Adopted Leader

_____

_____

Praise & Prayer for Today's FREEDOM SEVEN (See Chapter 11.)
Praise & Prayer for My Family

132

DAY 15—DATE _____
LOVING HIS WORD: HUMILITY

LUKE 18:10-14 (THE MESSAGE)

Two men went up to the Temple to pray, one a Pharisee, the other a tax man. The Pharisee posed and prayed like this: 'Oh, God, I thank you that I am not like other people—robbers, crooks, adulterers, or, heaven forbid, like this tax man. I fast twice a week and tithe on all my income.' Meanwhile the tax man, slumped in the shadows, his face in his hands, not daring to look up, said, 'God, give mercy. Forgive me, a sinner.'" Jesus commented, "This tax man, not the other, went home made right with God. If you walk around with your nose in the air, you're going to end up flat on your face, but if you're content to be simply yourself, you will become more than yourself."

PRAISING & PRAYING HIS WORD

Specific Need or Event: _____

Praise & Prayer for President Donald Trump

_____

_____

Praise & Prayer for Vice President Mike Pence

_____

_____

Praise & Prayer for Secretary of State Rex Tillerson

_____

_____

Praise & Prayer for Attorney General Jeff Sessions

_____

_____

Praise & Prayer for My Adopted Leader

_____

_____

Praise & Prayer for Today's FREEDOM SEVEN (See Chapter 11.)
Praise & Prayer for My Family

Day 16—Date _____
LOVING HIS WORD: Self-Control

Isaiah 55:6 (The Message)

Seek God while he's here to be found, pray to him while he's close at hand. Let the wicked abandon their way of life and the evil their way of thinking. Let them come back to God, who is merciful, come back to our God, who is lavish with forgiveness.

PRAISING & PRAYING HIS WORD

Specific Need or Event: _____

Praise & Prayer for President Donald Trump

_____

_____

Praise & Prayer for Vice President Mike Pence

_____

_____

Praise & Prayer for Secretary of State Rex Tillerson

_____

_____

Praise & Prayer for Attorney General Jeff Sessions

_____

_____

Praise & Prayer for My Adopted Leader

_____

_____

Praise & Prayer for Today's FREEDOM SEVEN (See Chapter 11.)

Praise & Prayer for My Family

DAY 17—DATE _____
LOVING HIS WORD: HOLD ON TO ROPE OF HOPE

MATTHEW 7:7-11 (THE MESSAGE)

Don't bargain with God. Be direct. Ask for what you need. This isn't a cat-and-mouse, hide-and-seek game we're in. If your child asks for bread, do you trick him with sawdust? If he asks for fish, do you scare him with a live snake on his plate? As bad as you are, you wouldn't think of such a thing. You're at least decent to your own children. So don't you think the God who conceived you in love will be even better?

PRAISING & PRAYING HIS WORD

Specific Need or Event: _____

Praise & Prayer for President Donald Trump

_____

_____

Praise & Prayer for Vice President Mike Pence

_____

_____

Praise & Prayer for Secretary of State Rex Tillerson

_____

_____

Praise & Prayer for Attorney General Jeff Sessions

_____

_____

Praise & Prayer for My Adopted Leader

_____

_____

Praise & Prayer for Today's FREEDOM SEVEN (See Chapter 11.)
Praise & Prayer for My Family

DAY 18—DATE _____
LOVING HIS WORD: GOD-LISTENING HEART

1 KINGS 3:9-14 (THE MESSAGE)

Here's what I want: Give me a God-listening heart so I can lead your people well, discerning the difference between good and evil. For who on their own is capable of leading your glorious people?"⁴ God, the Master, was delighted with Solomon's response. And God said to him, "Because you have asked for this and haven't grasped after a long life, or riches, or the doom of your enemies, but you have asked for the ability to lead and govern well, I'll give you what you've asked for—I'm giving you a wise and mature heart.

PRAISING & PRAYING HIS WORD

Specific Need or Event: _____

Praise & Prayer for President Donald Trump

_____

_____

Praise & Prayer for Vice President Mike Pence

_____

_____

Praise & Prayer for Secretary of State Rex Tillerson

_____

_____

Praise & Prayer for Attorney General Jeff Sessions

_____

_____

Praise & Prayer for My Adopted Leader

_____

_____

Praise & Prayer for Today's FREEDOM SEVEN (See Chapter 11.)
Praise & Prayer for My Family

136

DAY 19—DATE _____
LOVING HIS WORD: STRENGTH AND SONG

ISAIAH 12:1-2 (THE MESSAGE)

And you will say in that day, "I thank you, God. You were angry but your anger wasn't forever. You withdrew your anger and moved in and comforted me. "Yes, indeed—God is my salvation. I trust, I won't be afraid. God—yes God!—is my strength and song, best of all, my salvation!"

PRAISING & PRAYING HIS WORD

Specific Need or Event: _____

Praise & Prayer for President Donald Trump

_____

_____

Praise & Prayer for Vice President Mike Pence

_____

_____

Praise & Prayer for Secretary of State Rex Tillerson

_____

_____

Praise & Prayer for Attorney General Jeff Sessions

_____

_____

Praise & Prayer for My Adopted Leader

_____

_____

Praise & Prayer for Today's FREEDOM SEVEN (See Chapter 11.)

Praise & Prayer for My Family

DAY 20—DATE _____
LOVING HIS WORD: COMMITMENT TO PURITY

JAMES 4:10 (THE MESSAGE)

So let God work his will in you. Yell a loud *no* to the Devil and watch him scamper. Say a quiet *yes* to God and he'll be there in no time. Quit dabbling in sin. Purify your inner life. Quit playing the field. Hit bottom, and cry your eyes out. The fun and games are over. Get serious, really serious. Get down on your knees before the Master; it's the only way you'll get on your feet.

PRAISING & PRAYING HIS WORD

Specific Need or Event: _____

Praise & Prayer for President Donald Trump

_____

_____

Praise & Prayer for Vice President Mike Pence

_____

_____

Praise & Prayer for Secretary of State Rex Tillerson

_____

_____

Praise & Prayer for Attorney General Jeff Sessions

_____

_____

Praise & Prayer for My Adopted Leader

_____

_____

Praise & Prayer for Today's FREEDOM SEVEN (See Chapter 11.)
Praise & Prayer for My Family

Day 21—Date _____
LOVING HIS WORD: Be a Strong Christ Model

Colossians 1:9-12 (The Message)

Be assured that from the first day we heard of you, we haven't stopped praying for you, asking God to give you wise minds and spirits attuned to his will, and so acquire a thorough understanding of the ways in which God works. We pray that you'll live well for the Master, making him proud of you as you work hard in his orchard. As you learn more and more how God works, you will learn how to do *your* work. We pray that you'll have the strength to stick it out over the long haul—not the grim strength of gritting your teeth but the glory-strength God gives. It is strength that endures the unendurable and spills over into joy, thanking the Father who makes us strong enough to take part in everything bright and beautiful that he has for us.

PRAISING & PRAYING HIS WORD

Specific Need or Event: _____

Praise & Prayer for President Donald Trump

_____

_____

Praise & Prayer for Vice President Mike Pence

_____

_____

Praise & Prayer for Secretary of State Rex Tillerson

_____

_____

Praise & Prayer for Attorney General Jeff Sessions

_____

_____

Praise & Prayer for My Adopted Leader

_____

_____

Praise & Prayer for Today's FREEDOM SEVEN (See Chapter 11.)
Praise & Prayer for My Family

139

DAY 22—DATE _____
LOVING HIS WORD: LEARN TO THINK LIKE JESUS

1 PETER 4:2-7 (THE MESSAGE)

Since Jesus went through everything you're going through and more, learn to think like him. Think of your sufferings as a weaning from that old sinful habit of always expecting to get your own way. Then you'll be able to live out your days free to pursue what God wants instead of being tyrannized by what you want.[7] You've already put in your time in that God-ignorant way of life, partying night after night, a drunken and profligate life. Now it's time to be done with it for good. Of course, your old friends don't understand why you don't join in with the old gang anymore. But you don't have to give an account to them. They're the ones who will be called on the carpet—and before God himself.

PRAISING & PRAYING HIS WORD

Specific Need or Event: _____

Praise & Prayer for President Donald Trump

_____

_____

Praise & Prayer for Vice President Mike Pence

_____

_____

Praise & Prayer for Secretary of State Rex Tillerson

_____

_____

Praise & Prayer for Attorney General Jeff Sessions

_____

_____

Praise & Prayer for My Adopted Leader

_____

_____

Praise & Prayer for Today's FREEDOM SEVEN (See Chapter 11.)
Praise & Prayer for My Family

LOVING HIS WORD: FITNESS - SPIRITUAL AND PHYSICAL

2 THESSALONIANS 1:11-12 (THE MESSAGE)

Because we know that this extraordinary day is just ahead, we pray for you all the time—pray that our God will make you fit for what he's called you to be, pray that he'll fill your good ideas and acts of faith with his own energy so that it all amounts to something. If your life honors the name of Jesus, he will honor you. Grace is behind and through all of this, our God giving himself freely, the Master, Jesus Christ, giving himself freely.

PRAISING & PRAYING HIS WORD

Specific Need or Event: _____

Praise & Prayer for President Donald Trump

_____

_____

Praise & Prayer for Vice President Mike Pence

_____

_____

Praise & Prayer for Secretary of State Rex Tillerson

_____

_____

Praise & Prayer for Attorney General Jeff Sessions

_____

_____

Praise & Prayer for My Adopted Leader

_____

_____

Praise & Prayer for Today's FREEDOM SEVEN (See Chapter 11.)

Praise & Prayer for My Family

Day 24—Date _____
LOVING HIS WORD: Seek and Stand with God

1 Chronicles 16:10-19 (The Message)

Thank God! Call out his Name! Tell the whole world who he is and what he's Sing to him! Play songs for him! Broadcast all his wonders! Revel in his holy Name, God-seekers, be jubilant! Study God and his strength, seek his presence day and night; Remember all the wonders he performed, the miracles and judgments that came out of his mouth. Seed of Israel his servant! Children of Jacob, his first choice! He is God, *our* God; wherever you go you come on his judgments and decisions. He keeps his commitments across thousands of generations, the covenant he commanded.

PRAISING & PRAYING HIS WORD

Specific Need or Event: _____

Praise & Prayer for President Donald Trump

_____

_____

Praise & Prayer for Vice President Mike Pence

_____

_____

Praise & Prayer for Secretary of State Rex Tillerson

_____

_____

Praise & Prayer for Attorney General Jeff Sessions

_____

_____

Praise & Prayer for My Adopted Leader

_____

_____

Praise & Prayer for Today's FREEDOM SEVEN (See Chapter 11.)
Praise & Prayer for My Family

DAY 25—DATE _____
LOVING HIS WORD: EFFECTIVE LEADERSHIP

ROMANS 13:1-7 (THE MESSAGE)

Be a good citizen. All governments are under God. Insofar as there is peace and order, it's God's order. So live responsibly as a citizen. If you're irresponsible to the state, then you're irresponsible with God, and God will hold you responsible. Decent citizens should have nothing to fear. Do you want to be on good terms with the government? Be a responsible citizen and you'll get on just fine, the government working to your advantage. But if you're breaking the rules right and left, watch out. God also has an interest in keeping order, and he uses them to do it. That's why you must live responsibly—not just to avoid punishment but also because it's the right way to live. That's also why you pay taxes—so that an orderly way of life can be maintained. Fulfill your obligations as a citizen. Pay your taxes, pay your bills, respect your leaders.

PRAISING & PRAYING HIS WORD

Specific Need or Event: _____

Praise & Prayer for President Donald Trump

_____

_____

Praise & Prayer for Vice President Mike Pence

_____

_____

Praise & Prayer for Secretary of State Rex Tillerson

_____

_____

Praise & Prayer for Attorney General Jeff Sessions

_____

_____

Praise & Prayer for My Adopted Leader

_____

_____

Praise & Prayer for Today's FREEDOM SEVEN (See Chapter 11.)
Praise & Prayer for My Family

DAY 26—DATE _____
LOVING HIS WORD: FAITHFUL IN LISTENING & TALKING

LUKE 18:1-8 (THE MESSAGE)

Jesus told them a story showing that it was necessary for them to pray consistently and never quit. He said, "There was once a judge in some city who never gave God a thought and cared nothing for people. A widow in that city kept after him: 'My rights are being violated. Protect me!' He never gave her the time of day. But after this went on and on he said to himself, 'I care nothing what God thinks, even less what people think. But because this widow won't quit badgering me, I'd better do something and see that she gets justice—otherwise I'm going to end up beaten black-and-blue by her pounding.'" Then the Master said, "Do you hear what that judge, corrupt as he is, is saying? So what makes you think God won't step in and work justice for his chosen people, who continue to cry out for help? Won't he stick up for them? I assure you, he will. He will not drag his feet."

PRAISING & PRAYING HIS WORD

Specific Need or Event: _____

Praise & Prayer for President Donald Trump

_____

Praise & Prayer for Vice President Mike Pence

_____

Praise & Prayer for Secretary of State Rex Tillerson

_____

Praise & Prayer for Attorney General Jeff Sessions

_____

Praise & Prayer for My Adopted Leader

_____

Praise & Prayer for Today's FREEDOM SEVEN (See Chapter 11.)
Praise & Prayer for My Family

DAY 27—DATE _____
LOVING HIS WORD: ETHICAL INTEGRITY

HEBREWS 13:18 (THE MESSAGE)

Pray for us. We have no doubts about what we're doing or why, but it's hard going and we need your prayers. All we care about is living well before God. Pray that we may be together soon. May God, who puts all things together, makes all things whole, Who made a lasting mark through the sacrifice of Jesus, the sacrifice of blood that sealed the eternal covenant, Who led Jesus, our Great Shepherd, up and alive from the dead, Now put you together, provide you with everything you need to please him, Make us into what gives him most pleasure, by means of the sacrifice of Jesus, the Messiah. All glory to Jesus forever and always! Oh, yes, yes, yes!

PRAISING & PRAYING HIS WORD

Specific Need or Event: _____

Praise & Prayer for President Donald Trump

_____

_____

Praise & Prayer for Vice President Mike Pence

_____

_____

Praise & Prayer for Secretary of State Rex Tillerson

_____

_____

Praise & Prayer for Attorney General Jeff Sessions

_____

_____

Praise & Prayer for My Adopted Leader

_____

_____

Praise & Prayer for Today's FREEDOM SEVEN (See Chapter 11.)
Praise & Prayer for My Family

145

DAY 28—DATE _____
LOVING HIS WORD: TIME WITH THE FATHER

JOHN 14:10-14 (THE MESSAGE)

The person who trusts me will not only do what I'm doing but even greater things, because I, on my way to the Father, am giving you the same work to do that I've been doing. You can count on it. From now on, whatever you request along the lines of who I am and what I am doing, I'll do it. That's how the Father will be seen for who he is in the Son. I mean it. Whatever you request in this way, I'll do.

PRAISING & PRAYING HIS WORD

Specific Need or Event: _____

Praise & Prayer for President Donald Trump

_____

_____

Praise & Prayer for Vice President Mike Pence

_____

_____

Praise & Prayer for Secretary of State Rex Tillerson

_____

_____

Praise & Prayer for Attorney General Jeff Sessions

_____

_____

Praise & Prayer for My Adopted Leader

_____

_____

Praise & Prayer for Today's FREEDOM SEVEN (See Chapter 11.)
Praise & Prayer for My Family

DAY 29—DATE _____
LOVING HIS WORD: TRUSTING AND HOLDING ON

HEBREWS 4:12-16 (THE MESSAGE)

God means what he says. What he says goes. His powerful Word is sharp as a surgeon's scalpel, cutting through everything, whether doubt or defense, laying us open to listen and obey. Nothing and no one is impervious to God's Word. We can't get away from it—no matter what. Now that we know what we have—Jesus, this great High Priest with ready access to God—let's not let it slip through our fingers. We don't have a priest who is out of touch with our reality. He's been through weakness and testing, experienced it all—all but the sin. So let's walk right up to him and get what he is so ready to give. Take the mercy, accept the help.

PRAISING & PRAYING HIS WORD

Specific Need or Event: _____

Praise & Prayer for President Donald Trump

_____

_____

Praise & Prayer for Vice President Mike Pence

_____

_____

Praise & Prayer for Secretary of State Rex Tillerson

_____

_____

Praise & Prayer for Attorney General Jeff Sessions

_____

_____

Praise & Prayer for My Adopted Leader

_____

_____

Praise & Prayer for Today's FREEDOM SEVEN (See Chapter 11.)
Praise & Prayer for My Family

DAY 30—DATE _____
LOVING HIS WORD: Honor God and Nation

Psalm 11:1-7 (The Message)

I've already run for dear life straight to the arms of God. So why would I run away now when you say, "Run to the mountains; the evil bows are bent, the wicked arrows Aimed to shoot under cover of darkness at every heart open to God. The bottom's dropped out of the country; good people don't have a chance"? But God hasn't moved to the mountains; his holy address hasn't changed. He's in charge, as always, his eyes taking everything in, his eyelids Unblinking not missing a thing. He tests the good and the bad alike…God's business is putting things right; he loves getting the lines straight, setting us straight. Once we're standing tall, we can look him straight in the eye.

PRAISING & PRAYING HIS WORD

Specific Need or Event: _____

Praise & Prayer for President Donald Trump

_____

_____

Praise & Prayer for Vice President Mike Pence

_____

_____

Praise & Prayer for Secretary of State Rex Tillerson

_____

_____

Praise & Prayer for Attorney General Jeff Sessions

_____

_____

Praise & Prayer for My Adopted Leader

_____

_____

Praise & Prayer for Today's FREEDOM SEVEN (See Chapter 11.)
Praise & Prayer for My Family

DAY 31—DATE _____
LOVING HIS WORD: WALK IN FAITH AND TRUST

1 JOHN 5:13-15 (THE MESSAGE)

My purpose in writing is simply this: that you who believe in God's Son will know beyond the shadow of a doubt that you have eternal life, the reality and not the illusion. And how bold and free we then become in his presence, freely asking according to his will, sure that he's listening. And if we're confident that he's listening, we know that what we've asked for is as good as ours.

PRAISING & PRAYING HIS WORD

Specific Need or Event: _____

Praise & Prayer for President Donald Trump

_____

_____

Praise & Prayer for Vice President Mike Pence

_____

_____

Praise & Prayer for Secretary of State Rex Tillerson

_____

_____

Praise & Prayer for Attorney General Jeff Sessions

_____

_____

Praise & Prayer for My Adopted Leader

_____

_____

Praise & Prayer for Today's FREEDOM SEVEN (See Chapter 11.)

Praise & Prayer for My Family

Day 32—Date _____
LOVING HIS WORD: Godly Discernment

Romans 12:8-13 (The Message)

If you preach, just preach God's Message, nothing else; if you help, just help, don't take over; if you teach, stick to your teaching; if you give encouraging guidance, be careful that you don't get bossy; if you're put in charge, don't manipulate; if you're called to give aid to people in distress, keep your eyes open and be quick to respond; if you work with the disadvantaged, don't let yourself get irritated with them or depressed by them. Keep a smile on your face. Love from the center of who you are; don't fake it. Run for dear life from evil; hold on for dear life to good. Be good friends who love deeply; practice playing second fiddle. Don't burn out; keep yourselves fueled and aflame. Be alert servants of the Master, cheerfully expectant. Don't quit in hard times; pray all the harder. Help needy Christians; be inventive in hospitality.

PRAISING & PRAYING HIS WORD

Specific Need or Event: _____

Praise & Prayer for President Donald Trump

_____

_____

Praise & Prayer for Vice President Mike Pence

_____

_____

Praise & Prayer for Secretary of State Rex Tillerson

_____

_____

Praise & Prayer for Attorney General Jeff Sessions

_____

_____

Praise & Prayer for My Adopted Leader

_____

_____

Praise & Prayer for Today's FREEDOM SEVEN (See Chapter 11.)
Praise & Prayer for My Family

Day 33—Date _____
LOVING HIS WORD: Abide in Christ

John 14:1-7 (The Message)

Don't let this throw you. You trust God, don't you? Trust me. There is plenty of room for you in my Father's home. If that weren't so, would I have told you that I'm on my way to get a room ready for you? And if I'm on my way to get your room ready, I'll come back and get you so you can live where I live. And you already know the road I'm taking. Thomas said, "Master, we have no idea where you're going. How do you expect us to know the road?" Jesus said, "I am the Road, also the Truth, also the Life. No one gets to the Father apart from me. If you really knew me, you would know my Father as well. From now on, you do know him. You've even seen him!"

PRAISING & PRAYING HIS WORD

Specific Need or Event: _____

Praise & Prayer for President Donald Trump

_____

_____

Praise & Prayer for Vice President Mike Pence

_____

_____

Praise & Prayer for Secretary of State Rex Tillerson

_____

_____

Praise & Prayer for Attorney General Jeff Sessions

_____

_____

Praise & Prayer for My Adopted Leader

_____

_____

Praise & Prayer for Today's FREEDOM SEVEN (See Chapter 11.)
Praise & Prayer for My Family

DAY 34—DATE _____
LOVING HIS WORD: CRY OUT TO GOD

2 CHRONICLES 7:13-16 (THE MESSAGE)

If I ever shut off the supply of rain from the skies or order the locusts to eat the crops or send a plague on my people, and my people, my God-defined people, respond by humbling themselves, praying, seeking my presence, and turning their backs on their wicked lives, I'll be there ready for you: I'll listen from heaven, forgive their sins, and restore their land to health. From now on I'm alert day and night to the prayers offered at this place. Believe me, I've chosen and sanctified this Temple that you have built: My Name is stamped on it forever; my eyes are on it and my heart in it always.

PRAISING & PRAYING HIS WORD

Specific Need or Event: _____

Praise & Prayer for President Donald Trump

_____

_____

Praise & Prayer for Vice President Mike Pence

_____

_____

Praise & Prayer for Secretary of State Rex Tillerson

_____

_____

Praise & Prayer for Attorney General Jeff Sessions

_____

_____

Praise & Prayer for My Adopted Leader

_____

_____

Praise & Prayer for Today's FREEDOM SEVEN (See Chapter 11.)
Praise & Prayer for My Family

DAY 35—DATE _____
LOVING HIS WORD: Live Wisely

PROVERBS 3:30-35 (THE MESSAGE)

Don't walk around with a chip on your shoulder, always spoiling for a fight. Don't try to be like those who shoulder their way through life. Why be a bully? "Why not?" you say. Because God can't stand twisted souls. It's the straightforward who get his respect.33-35 God's curse blights the house of the wicked, but he blesses the home of the righteous. He gives proud skeptics a cold shoulder, but if you're down on your luck, he's right there to help. Wise living gets rewarded with honor; stupid living gets the booby prize.

PRAISING & PRAYING HIS WORD

Specific Need or Event: _____

Praise & Prayer for President Donald Trump

_____

_____

Praise & Prayer for Vice President Mike Pence

_____

_____

Praise & Prayer for Secretary of State Rex Tillerson

_____

_____

Praise & Prayer for Attorney General Jeff Sessions

_____

_____

Praise & Prayer for My Adopted Leader

_____

_____

Praise & Prayer for Today's FREEDOM SEVEN (See Chapter 11.)
Praise & Prayer for My Family

DAY 36—DATE _____
LOVING HIS WORD: RESIST EVIL PLOY

1 CORINTHIANS 10:11-13 (THE MESSAGE)

These are all warning markers—danger!—in our history books, written down so that we don't repeat their mistakes. Our positions in the story are parallel—they at the beginning, we at the end—and we are just as capable of messing it up as they were. Don't be so naive and self-confident. You're not exempt. You could fall flat on your face as easily as anyone else. Forget about self-confidence; it's useless. Cultivate God-confidence. No test or temptation that comes your way is beyond the course of what others have had to face. All you need to remember is that God will never let you down; he'll never let you be pushed past your limit; he'll always be there to help you come through it.

PRAISING & PRAYING HIS WORD

Specific Need or Event: _____

Praise & Prayer for President Donald Trump

_____

_____

Praise & Prayer for Vice President Mike Pence

_____

_____

Praise & Prayer for Secretary of State Rex Tillerson

_____

_____

Praise & Prayer for Attorney General Jeff Sessions

_____

_____

Praise & Prayer for My Adopted Leader

_____

_____

Praise & Prayer for Today's FREEDOM SEVEN (See Chapter 11.)
Praise & Prayer for My Family

DAY 37—DATE _____
LOVING HIS WORD: DEPEND ON THE HOLY SPIRIT

ROMANS 12:9-13 (THE MESSAGE)

Love from the center of who you are; don't fake it. Run for dear life from evil; hold on for dear life to good. Be good friends who love deeply; practice playing second fiddle. Don't burn out; keep yourselves fueled and aflame. Be alert servants of the Master, cheerfully expectant. Don't quit in hard times; pray all the harder. Help needy Christians; be inventive in hospitality.

PRAISING & PRAYING HIS WORD

Specific Need or Event: _____

Praise & Prayer for President Donald Trump

_____

_____

Praise & Prayer for Vice President Mike Pence

_____

_____

Praise & Prayer for Secretary of State Rex Tillerson

_____

_____

Praise & Prayer for Attorney General Jeff Sessions

_____

_____

Praise & Prayer for My Adopted Leader

_____

_____

Praise & Prayer for Today's FREEDOM SEVEN (See Chapter 11.)
Praise & Prayer for My Family

DAY 38—DATE _____
LOVING HIS WORD: PRIORITY - FIRST THINGS FIRST

LUKE 12:9-12 (THE MESSAGE)

Stand up for me among the people you meet and the Son of Man will stand up for you before all God's angels. But if you pretend you don't know me, do you think I'll defend you before God's angels? If you bad-mouth the Son of Man out of misunderstanding or ignorance, that can be overlooked. But if you're knowingly attacking God himself, taking aim at the Holy Spirit, that won't be overlooked. When they drag you into their meeting places, or into police courts and before judges, don't worry about defending yourselves—what you'll say or how you'll say it. The right words will be there. The Holy Spirit will give you the right words when the time comes.

PRAISING & PRAYING HIS WORD

Specific Need or Event: _____

Praise & Prayer for President Donald Trump

_____

_____

Praise & Prayer for Vice President Mike Pence

_____

_____

Praise & Prayer for Secretary of State Rex Tillerson

_____

_____

Praise & Prayer for Attorney General Jeff Sessions

_____

_____

Praise & Prayer for My Adopted Leader

_____

_____

Praise & Prayer for Today's FREEDOM SEVEN (See Chapter 11.)
Praise & Prayer for My Family

DAY 39—DATE _____
LOVING HIS WORD: A MIGHTY FORCE IN GOD'S HANDS

MATTHEW 6:7 (THE MESSAGE)

The world is full of so-called prayer warriors who are prayer-ignorant. They're full of formulas and programs and advice, peddling techniques for getting what you want from God. Don't fall for that nonsense. This is your Father you are dealing with, and he knows better than you what you need. With a God like this loving you, you can pray very simply.

PRAISING & PRAYING HIS WORD

Specific Need or Event: _____

Praise & Prayer for President Donald Trump

_____

_____

Praise & Prayer for Vice President Mike Pence

_____

_____

Praise & Prayer for Secretary of State Rex Tillerson

_____

_____

Praise & Prayer for Attorney General Jeff Sessions

_____

_____

Praise & Prayer for My Adopted Leader

_____

_____

Praise & Prayer for Today's FREEDOM SEVEN (See Chapter 11.)
Praise & Prayer for My Family

DAY 40—DATE _____
LOVING HIS WORD: Measure Treasure

MATTHEW 6:2-4 (THE MESSAGE)

When you do something for someone else, don't call attention to yourself. You've seen them in action, I'm sure—'play actors' I call them—treating prayer meeting and street corner alike as a stage, acting compassionate as long as someone is watching, playing to the crowds. They get applause, true, but that's all they get. When you help someone out, don't think about how it looks. Just do it—quietly and unobtrusively. That is the way your God, who conceived you in love, working behind the scenes, helps you out.

PRAISING & PRAYING HIS WORD

Specific Need or Event: _____

Praise & Prayer for President Donald Trump

_____

_____

Praise & Prayer for Vice President Mike Pence

_____

_____

Praise & Prayer for Secretary of State Rex Tillerson

_____

_____

Praise & Prayer for Attorney General Jeff Sessions

_____

_____

Praise & Prayer for My Adopted Leader

_____

_____

Praise & Prayer for Today's FREEDOM SEVEN (See Chapter 11.)
Praise & Prayer for My Family

DAY 41—DATE _____
LOVING HIS WORD: SHARE LOVE AND FAITH

MATTHEW 28:19 19 (THE MESSAGE)

Get Up! Get Out! Go Tell:

Jesus, undeterred, went right ahead and gave his charge: "God authorized and commanded me to commission you: Go out and train everyone you meet, far and near, in this way of life, marking them by baptism in the threefold name: Father, Son, and Holy Spirit. Then instruct them in the practice of all I have commanded you. I'll be with you as you do this, day after day after day, right up to the end of the age."

PRAISING & PRAYING HIS WORD

Specific Need or Event: _____

Praise & Prayer for President Donald Trump

_____

_____

Praise & Prayer for Vice President Mike Pence

_____

_____

Praise & Prayer for Secretary of State Rex Tillerson

_____

_____

Praise & Prayer for Attorney General Jeff Sessions

_____

_____

Praise & Prayer for My Adopted Leader

_____

_____

Praise & Prayer for Today's FREEDOM SEVEN (See Chapter 11.)
Praise & Prayer for My Family

DAY 42—DATE _____
LOVING HIS WORD: PRAY SIMPLE PRAYERS

MATTHEW 6:8-13 (THE MESSAGE)

Our Father in heaven, Reveal who you are. Set the world right; Do what's best— as above, so below. Keep us alive with three square meals. Keep us forgiven with you and forgiving others. Keep us safe from ourselves and the Devil. You're in charge! You can do anything you want! You're ablaze in beauty! Yes. Yes. Yes.

PRAISING & PRAYING HIS WORD

Specific Need or Event: _____

Praise & Prayer for President Donald Trump

_____

_____

Praise & Prayer for Vice President Mike Pence

_____

_____

Praise & Prayer for Secretary of State Rex Tillerson

_____

_____

Praise & Prayer for Attorney General Jeff Sessions

_____

_____

Praise & Prayer for My Adopted Leader

_____

_____

Praise & Prayer for Today's FREEDOM SEVEN (See Chapter 11.)

Praise & Prayer for My Family

DAY 43—DATE _____
LOVING HIS WORD: BLESS AND ENCOURAGE OTHERS

ROMANS 12:19-21 (THE MESSAGE)

Don't hit back; discover beauty in everyone. If you've got it in you, get along with everybody. Don't insist on getting even; that's not for you to do. "I'll do the judging, says God. "I'll take care of it." Our Scriptures tell us that if you see your enemy hungry, go buy that person lunch, or if he's thirsty, get him a drink. Your generosity will surprise him with goodness. Don't let evil get the best of you; get the best of evil by doing good.

PRAISING & PRAYING HIS WORD

Specific Need or Event: _____

Praise & Prayer for President Donald Trump

_____

_____

Praise & Prayer for Vice President Mike Pence

_____

_____

Praise & Prayer for Secretary of State Rex Tillerson

_____

_____

Praise & Prayer for Attorney General Jeff Sessions

_____

_____

Praise & Prayer for My Adopted Leader

_____

_____

Praise & Prayer for Today's FREEDOM SEVEN (See Chapter 11.)

Praise & Prayer for My Family

DAY 44—DATE _____
LOVING HIS WORD: SEEK GOD'S BEST

MATTHEW 6:31 (THE MESSAGE)

If God gives such attention to the appearance of wildflowers—most of which are never even seen—don't you think he'll attend to you, take pride in you, do his best for you? What I'm trying to do here is to get you to relax, to not be so preoccupied with *getting*, so you can respond to God's *giving*. People who don't know God and the way he works fuss over these things, but you know both God and how he works. Steep your life in God-reality, God-initiative, God-provisions. Don't worry about missing out. You'll find all your everyday human concerns will be met.

PRAISING & PRAYING HIS WORD

Specific Need or Event: _____

Praise & Prayer for President Donald Trump

_____

_____

Praise & Prayer for Vice President Mike Pence

_____

_____

Praise & Prayer for Secretary of State Rex Tillerson

_____

_____

Praise & Prayer for Attorney General Jeff Sessions

_____

_____

Praise & Prayer for My Adopted Leader

_____

_____

Praise & Prayer for Today's FREEDOM SEVEN (See Chapter 11.)
Praise & Prayer for My Family

DAY 45—DATE _____
LOVING HIS WORD: Seek His Rest

PSALM 23 (THE MESSAGE)

God, my shepherd! I don't need a thing. You have bedded me down in lush meadows, you find me quiet pools to drink from. True to your word, you let me catch my breath and send me in the right direction. Even when the way goes through Death Valley, I'm not afraid when you walk at my side. Your trusty shepherd's crook makes me feel secure. You serve me a six-course dinner right in front of my enemies. You revive my drooping head; my cup brims with blessing. Your beauty and love chase after me every day of my life. I'm back home in the house of God for the rest of my life.

PRAISING & PRAYING HIS WORD

Specific Need or Event: _____

Praise & Prayer for President Donald Trump

_____

_____

Praise & Prayer for Vice President Mike Pence

_____

_____

Praise & Prayer for Secretary of State Rex Tillerson

_____

_____

Praise & Prayer for Attorney General Jeff Sessions

_____

_____

Praise & Prayer for My Adopted Leader

_____

_____

Praise & Prayer for Today's FREEDOM SEVEN (See Chapter 11.)
Praise & Prayer for My Family

163

LOVING HIS WORD: CLAIM HIS YES PROMISES

2 CORINTHIANS 1:20 (THE MESSAGE)

Whatever God has promised gets stamped with the Yes of Jesus. In him, this is what we preach and pray, the great Amen, God's Yes, and our Yes together, gloriously evident. God affirms us, making us a sure thing in Christ, putting his Yes within us. By his Spirit he has stamped us with his eternal pledge—a sure beginning of what he is destined to complete.

PRAISING & PRAYING HIS WORD

Specific Need or Event: _____

Praise & Prayer for President Donald Trump

_____

_____

Praise & Prayer for Vice President Mike Pence

_____

_____

Praise & Prayer for Secretary of State Rex Tillerson

_____

_____

Praise & Prayer for Attorney General Jeff Sessions

_____

_____

Praise & Prayer for My Adopted Leader

_____

_____

Praise & Prayer for Today's FREEDOM SEVEN (See Chapter 11.)
Praise & Prayer for My Family

Day 47—Date _____
LOVING HIS WORD: Hold on to Rope of Hope

Hebrews 10:23 (The Message)

So let's *do* it—full of belief, confident that we're presentable inside and out. Let's keep a firm grip on the promises that keep us going. He always keeps his word. Let's see how inventive we can be in encouraging love and helping out, not avoiding worshiping together as some do but spurring each other on, especially as we see the big Day approaching.

PRAISING & PRAYING HIS WORD

Specific Need or Event: _____

Praise & Prayer for President Donald Trump

_____

_____

Praise & Prayer for Vice President Mike Pence

_____

_____

Praise & Prayer for Secretary of State Rex Tillerson

_____

_____

Praise & Prayer for Attorney General Jeff Sessions

_____

_____

Praise & Prayer for My Adopted Leader

_____

_____

Praise & Prayer for Today's FREEDOM SEVEN (See Chapter 11.)

Praise & Prayer for My Family

DAY 48—DATE _____
LOVING HIS WORD: LOVE LIKE JESUS

2 THESSALONIANS 2:16-17 (THE MESSAGE)

So, friends, take a firm stand, feet on the ground and head high. Keep a tight grip on what you were taught, whether in personal conversation or by our letter. May Jesus himself and God our Father, who reached out in love and surprised you with gifts of unending help and confidence, put a fresh heart in you, invigorate your work, enliven your speech.

PRAISING & PRAYING HIS WORD

Specific Need or Event: _____

Praise & Prayer for President Donald Trump

_____

_____

Praise & Prayer for Vice President Mike Pence

_____

_____

Praise & Prayer for Secretary of State Rex Tillerson

_____

_____

Praise & Prayer for Attorney General Jeff Sessions

_____

_____

Praise & Prayer for My Adopted Leader

_____

_____

Praise & Prayer for Today's FREEDOM SEVEN (See Chapter 11.)
Praise & Prayer for My Family

Day 26—Date _____
LOVING HIS WORD: Stand Up! Praise & Applaud God

Psalm 100 (The Message)

On your feet now—applaud God! Bring a gift of laughter, sing yourselves into his presence.[3] Know this: God is God, and God, God. He made us; we didn't make him. We're his people, his well-tended sheep. Enter with the password: PRAISE: Thank you! Make yourselves at home, talking praise. Thank him. Worship him. For God is sheer beauty, all-generous in love, loyal always and ever.

PRAISING & PRAYING HIS WORD

Specific Need or Event: _____

Praise & Prayer for President Donald Trump

_____

_____

Praise & Prayer for Vice President Mike Pence

_____

_____

Praise & Prayer for Secretary of State Rex Tillerson

_____

_____

Praise & Prayer for Attorney General Jeff Sessions

_____

_____

Praise & Prayer for My Adopted Leader

_____

_____

Praise & Prayer for Today's FREEDOM SEVEN (See Chapter 11.)
Praise & Prayer for My Family

UNIT 9

GOD'S RESOURCES

Chapter 14

Apply for God's Supply

In the Old Testament, there were the political leaders — the kings, and the spiritual leaders — and the priests and prophets. While God allowed this, he rightfully reserved the Kingship for his son Jesus, who would bring perfect leadership to imperfect people.

After His people insisted on a king, to be like other nations, leadership fell under two separate administrations. These had separate roles and responsibilities.

The king was the political and military leader of the people — much like America today with our President and Commander-in-chief.

The priest and the prophets were the spiritual leaders of the people — much like the pastoral leader of a local church.

The governing of nations and the shepherding of the spiritual lives of people are two separate and distinct responsibilities, which God allowed to develop. In America we are part of that development as we have the right of choosing godly Leaders.

Samuel Adams said, "Let each citizen remember at the moment he is offering his vote that he is not making a present or a compliment to please an individual – or at least that he ought not so to do; but that he is executing one of the most solemn trusts in human society for which he is accountable to God and his country."

Today in America many people live with a spirit of entitlement. They look to the government to meet their need, or they look to God to fill their greed.

Under our Constitution, men and women are in office to live circumspectly with honor and respect as they provide positive leadership and preserve liberty for all to worship or not worship.

As Jesus Followers, and a nation built on biblical values and principles, it behooves us to have political leaders that have a personal

169

relationship with Jesus Christ. Leaders who live lives in accordance with God's Word, which was the ideal and established right provided by our Founding Fathers.

They set forth the way of blessing in giving us the reason to select and elect our governing leaders. The majority assumed and established the lifestyle of obedience and service to God.

Spiritual leaders are chosen, appointed and anointed by God to go forth to reach, teach and train others to lead by his Spirit. This raises the question: Whose responsibility is it that this nation's culture and society is in such disarray? What are we to do in that regard?

History would tell us both the political and spiritual leaders are faulty. Not all of them, but most of them. Add that to absentee parenting and the spirit of entitlement, and you have not just a loss of sacred trust, but life without liberty.

What has developed is a culture generated by two full generations who are un-churched and who chose to "live it my way."

Yet, people are looking for the answers to the issues of life. There are plenty of wrong answers.

The fastest growing movements in America today are the godless people in political parties, cults and false religions. They have captured the media with boldness taking lies and expectations directly to churched and un-churched people. Every day their influence is growing.

Jesus Followers believe God will hold accountable those whom He has called to spiritual leadership — from the breakfast tables, to the schools, to the pulpits of America.

The big questions are: Whom can we trust? Can we return to the faith and strength of the fathers who have given their lives for liberty? This is not a covered-wagon trip. It is one to the cross! To pray is to apply for his supply,

P. Present ourselves just as we are to God as living loving sacrifices.
> **Praise Him** that He is our need and supply and He is willing and able.

L. Listen to His voice as we love others and seek Him.
> **Learn from** His Word and Spirit how to submit to Him and be leaders that people can follow to Jesus.

Y. Yield to His will and way as we trust Him and believe.

      Yearn for his heart for life, liberty and pursuit of happiness.

Join million across America and use this P.L.Y. principle to pray for the soul of America and our nation whose God is the Lord.

God is faithful to his promises. He says, "Call me and I *will* answer you and show you great and mighty wonders" (Jeremiah 33:3 NKJV).

Unit 10

God's Light for Salting

CHAPTER 15

PRAYER OF PRAISE

KING DAVID'S PRAYER OF PRAISE

You *are* right and you *do* right, GOD,
your decisions are right on target.
You rightly instruct us in how to live ever faithful to you.
My rivals nearly did me in,
they persistently ignored your commandments.
Your promise has been tested through and through,
and I, your servant, love it.
I'm too young to be important,
but I don't forget what you tell me.
Your righteousness is eternally right,
your revelation is the only truth.
Even though troubles came down on me hard,
your commands always gave me delight.
The way you tell me to live is always right;
help me understand it so I can live to the fullest.
I call out at the top of my lungs, "GOD! Answer!
I'll do whatever you say."
I called to you, "Save me so
I can carry out all your instructions."
In your love, listen to me; in your justice,
GOD, keep me alive.
Take a good look at my trouble, and help me —
I haven't forgotten your revelation.
Take my side and get me out of this;
give me back my life, just as you promised.
Psalm 119

MY PRAYER OF PRAISE

Heavenly Father, I surrender to You the burdens that I carry that You never intended for me to carry.

I cast all my cares upon You. My worries, fears, anxiety and sorrow. Your Word says I am not to be anxious about anything, but rather to bring everything to You in prayer and praise. I surrender.
Father, calm my broken heart and quiet my restless spirit. Still my troubling worries about our nation with Your assurance that You are in control of my life and our beloved America.

Father, help me turn loose of my grip on the things I am hanging onto as I come to You with open hands.

Father, I surrender to Your will all that I am trying to control and manage. Change my manipulating heart and will to Your will and way.

Father, I give to You all my plans and expectations and ask that You open my eyes to see You and hear you speak. I believe that I might receive Your answers and blessing.

Father, I praise you for all Your promises that are "*yes*" is Christ Jesus. I thank You for protection, peace, and provision.

Father, I pray in the powerful name of Your Son Jesus and surrender everything to Your will to be done in my life and America. Your Way! In the name of Jesus.

CHAPTER 16
THE FATHER'S LIGHT & SALT

With the God-given wisdom of our founding documents, God presented clear and certain ways for bringing changes when things are wrong in our beloved land.

All the resources of Almighty God and His Word are available to us. He rules in the affairs of men, and nothing is too hard for Him. He is the sovereign King of the universe, with all power and authority — and He is compassionate, gracious and ready to extend his love and mercy to those willing to obey and trust Him.

Let's bend our knees and humble our hearts and pray. Let's be willing to be used of God to help turn this nation back to him. Let's stand in the GAP: and seek Him to make us salt and light in our families, communities and workplaces.

God wants that for us. He came to forgive our sins and heal our nation as we pray and believe, we must take the following action.

LOVE JESUS
We spend time with God in prayer and communion because we love him. If we love God we will desire to be with Him and to fellowship with Him.

DEPEND ON JESUS
He is our source. He is our life (Colossians 3:4). Through prayer we receive the comfort, the strength and the other resources that we need in life – both naturally and spiritually. Prayer – relationship to God – is as necessary to the spiritual life as air to the natural life.

RESIST TEMPTATION
"Watch and pray, lest you enter into temptation." (Matthew 26:41). Much sin is the result of the sin of prayerlessness. Through lack of prayer, we are weak, others are weaker and Satan gains the advantage in our lives.

INVITE GOD TO ACT IN SALVATION

God gave the earth to Adam and his descendants. We must invite God to work here. If no-one invites God to work here, Satan (the god of this world through man's universal rebellion – Second Corinthians 4:4) will dominate the affairs of men and eventually the judgment of God will come.

PRAISE AND PRAY

"Continue earnestly in prayer, being vigilant in it with thanksgiving." (Colossians 4:2). "Then he [Jesus] spoke a parable to them to this end that men ought always to pray and not lose heart." (Luke 18:1). The need to pray is as great as the authority of God which commands us: "Pray without ceasing." (1 Thessalonians 5:17).

REMEMBER WHAT HE HAS DONE IN AMERICA

Praise him for what He will do today. As American troops stormed the beaches of Normandy, President Franklin Roosevelt called for our nation to unite in prayer. He also offered a prayer to prepare each citizen for the road ahead.

> "Let our hearts be stout, to wait out the long travail, to bear sorrows that may come, to impart our courage unto our sons where ever they may be. And, O Lord, give us faith. Give us faith in Thee."
> – FDR

Prayer must be for guidance, protection and strength.

> "It is the duty of nations, as well as men, to owe their dependence upon the overruling power of God."
> – Abraham Lincoln

Today the need for prayer is as great as ever. Our nation again faces battlefields, along with an epidemic of broken homes, violence, sexual immorality and social strife. We must ask the Lord to bless our leaders with wisdom and protection, and that we will have the fortitude to overcome the challenges at hand.

It is our goal that you, your family, and friends would participate in Praising & Praying Across America. We pray this book will impact your life and that praying for our nation moves from a 98-day project to a lifetime endeavor.

CHAPTER 17

LIGHT TO SHOW THE WAY OF SALT

SALT AND LIGHT

Weary and worn is the world today
with hopelessness in darkness lay.
All they like sheep have gone astray.
In need of light to show the way.
Desire for truth in the world is gone.
Lovers of self all have become.
How will they know unless someone will
share the news of the risen Son?

We are the salt and light with hope for a dying world
To preserve and show the right of a life within God's Word
So stand and join the fight. Will you heed the call?
We are the salt. We are the light.

We are not good on our own within.
We choose ourselves what we think is sin.
God's Word is clear we must begin to
live as salt and our world to win.

We are the salt and light with hope for a dying world
To preserve and show the right of a life within God's Word
So stand and join the fight. Will you heed the call?
We are the salt. We are the light.

As salt and light, it is not fate.
We have the choice, it's not too late.
The time is now, we cannot wait.
Our goal is truth and our path is straight.

We are the salt and light with hope for a dying world
To preserve and show the right of a life within God's Word
So stand and join the fight. Will you heed the call?
We are the salt. We are the light.

We are the salt and light with hope for a dying world
To preserve and show the right of a life within God's Word
So stand and join the fight. Will you heed the call?

We are the salt. We are the light.

We are the salt. We are the light.

MOVING FORWARD WITH JOY

If you are asked, 'What does Jesus' Love mean to you?' how would you answer?

If you think there is a God, but do not know, what is missing?

If your prayers are not being answered, what is wrong?

If your love walk is aimless, where are you going?

If your love talk is powerless, are you listening?

If you do not see God working, are you blinded?

If you journey is not one of joy, how can I get back?

If you don't know the answers to these questions, what should you do?

These questions raise issues that Jesus Christ alone can answer. His answers are in the Bible, which is his Word. The Father has vowed to hear your cries and answer if you seek him. He is constantly tuned to all who are seeking and searching for the answers to the issues of life. Jesus has qualified (made the way) for you to receive the gift of the Grace Life by giving his own life as a ransom for you — forgiving your unbelief and rebellion. It comes only one way — it is by new birth — not work.

Jesus says, "I have come that you might have life and have it to the full" (John 10:10 NIV). He wills to connect with you through the price He paid at Calvary and sealed at the empty tomb.

Jesus says, "You did not choose me, but I chose you and appointed you so that you might go and bear fruit—fruit that will last…." (John 15:16 NIV). He knows your street address, your cell number and post importantly your heart need. There are no secrets in his love plan.

The Father says, "I have so loved you, that I have given you my One and Only that if you will believe and receive him as my gift of life, you will not perish — but have everlasting life." (John 3:16 my paraphrase).

How can you receive this great gift? It is available and free for the asking — as simple as ABC.

A—Acknowledge that you are lost in the wilderness of the world's way, and you cannot change or forgive yourself. Accept his love and ask Him for his gift of life.

B—Believe that Jesus loves you enough that He gave his life as a ransom for you personally and believe that He has a plan for your life.

C—Confess Him as Lord and Savior as you believe in your heart. Jesus is: "The way, truth, and life," and there is no other way. Commit your life to seeking and living His love plan.

If you desire this gift, you can kneel and ask Jesus to forgive you and give you a new life — right now.

Jesus is calling each of us to get out of the prayer closets, report for active duty, and pray as we serve him and fight for Christ-centered values. When we pray, the Holy Spirit works. Through Jesus, therefore, let us continually offer to God a sacrifice of praise — the fruit of our lips that confess his name.

"May the God of peace, who through the blood of the eternal covenant brought back from the dead our Lord Jesus, the great Shepherd of the sheep, equip you with everything good for doing his will, and may He work in us what is pleasing to him, through Jesus Christ, to whom be glory for ever and ever. Amen" (Hebrews 13:20 NIV).

God's Word is powerful, and He desires to use it, and us, to make America great.

There is no greater glory that we can offer Jesus than a life that is qualified by His grace and occupied by His love, giving Him glory as we begin *Praising & Praying Across America.*

Let us begin to live so everyone can see our Lord's Love in us.

Onward in joy.

About Evelyn Davison

Evelyn Davison loves Texas and Texans and America and Americans. As a radio and TV personality, Evelyn has spread "Love Talk™" across the state and nation through the Love Talk Network, which she founded.

As a prayer warrior, Evelyn has prayed for and become the friend of presidents, governors, elected officials, pastors, and other leaders across the nation. Evelyn is Publisher for the *Good News Journal*, Central Texas' Christian Newspaper. Since 1974, Evelyn has given leadership to the annual observance of National Day of Prayer in Texas and was named America's Honorary Prayer Coordinator for NDP during George W. Bush's first term.

Evelyn is prayer coordinator for CLASSeminars and the CLASS Christian Writers Conference. She has written hundreds of magazine and newspaper articles and is a contributing author in numerous books.

Evelyn and her husband Van have two adult sons and make their home in Austin, Texas.

Contact Evelyn at

Email: evelyndavison@gmail.com

Address:
PO Box 170069
Austin, Texas 78717-0069

The Good News Journal: www.thegoodnewsjournal.net
Love Talk Network: www.lovetalknetwork.com
CLASS: www.classeminars.org
National Day of Prayer: www.nationaldayofprayer.org

ABOUT THE CO-AUTHORS

JOHN BORNSCHEIN

John Bornschein is the Vice Chairman of the National Day of Prayer Task Force and Senior Pastor of Calvary Fellowship Fountain Valley church. At 38 years of age, he and his wife, Brandi, have 5 children and together they have served in ministry for more than 20 years. To learn more, visit www.NationalDayofPrayer.org

ANNE GRAHAM LOTZ

Anne Graham Lotz, Chairman of National Day of Prayer, and an American Christian evangelist. She is the second daughter of evangelist Billy Graham and his wife Ruth Graham. She founded AnGel Ministries and is the author of 11 books. Her best known book is *Just Give Me Jesus*. www.AnneGrahamLotz.org

DR. STEVE WASHBURN

Dr. Washburn is Senior Pastor at First Baptist Church, Pflugerville, Texas. He earned his Master of Divinity and Doctor of Ministry degrees at Southwestern Baptist Theological Seminary in Ft. Worth.

Pastor Washburn serves in a leadership role in the Austin Baptist Association (ABA), and has previously served the Southern Baptist of Texas Convention (SBTC) and the Southern Baptist Convention (SBC).

GERRY WAKELAND

Gerry Wakeland is the President and CEO of CLASSEMINARS, Inc. a Christian training and equipping organization. She also serves on the staff of Albuquerque's First Baptist Church where she loves teaching discipleship to God's women. www.classeminars. org

DR. TREY KENT

Trey Kent started Northwest Fellowship in Austin, Texas, in 1993 and has been in full time ministry since 1986. He has a Masters of Divinity and Doctor of Ministry work at Fuller Seminary. His passions are Jesus, prayer, and his family. He is the proud husband of Mary Anne and the grateful father of daughters Lindsay, Christina and son in law, Nick. In 2009, God led Trey to launch the Unceasing Prayer Initiative mobilizing 40 churches to pray 24-7 for unity and revival in Austin. www.northwestfellowship. com

CAROL EVERETT

Carol Everett's life has been entrenched in women's reproductive health choices. Her unplanned pregnancy at age sixteen, six years of selling abortions to other women to justify her own, her part in thirty-five thousand abortions brought her to a crossroads where she experienced a live-altering change of salvation from Jesus Christ. She formed the Heidi Group which helps women and families secure life in Christ and economic stability. www.info@ heidigroup.org

REV. WAYNE WINSAUER

Rev. Wayne Winsauer is a graduate of Washington State University with a degree in Communications. He came face to face with Jesus at the age of 42 years. He and his wife Bunny have two daughters, five grandkids, and one great grandchild. The Winsauer's ministry includes Bible teaching on cruise ships around the world. www. forgodsglory777@q.com

DR. PHIL WARE

Phil Ware works with churches in transition with Interim Ministry Partners and for the past 18 years, has been editor and president of Heartlight Magazine. He is the author of Verseoftheday.com and a year with Jesus.com. Phil and Donna have two children, Zachary and Megan. They live in Abilene, Texas. Contact www. heartlight.org

LISA CRUMP

Lisa Crump serves as the Chief Operations Officer for the National Day of Prayer Task Force. Lisa completed her Bachelors in Organizational Management, Human Resources Emphasis from Colorado Christian University..

Lisa served at the international ministry of Focus on the Family for 10 years. There, she spent several years staffing employment positions for the ministry, then served as National Volunteer Coordinator for over 15 years.

In 2003 Lisa moved to National Day of Prayer Task Force under Chairman Mrs. Shirley Dobson. Today Lisa is the Chief Operations Officer under Ms. Anne Graham Lotz and serves with the nation-wide coordinator network consisting of thousands of volunteers across America working to call our nation to prayer. This network mobilizes prayer on the First Thursday of May annually through the federal statue, and throughout the year. Lisa and her husband   Mike live in Colorado Springs, and love spending time serving the Lord and loving on their family. www. nationaldayofprayer.org

REV. LINDA CHANDLER

Linda Chandler is the ordained pastor at Austin Brethren Church. Linda has a B.S.Ed from the University of Texas, a M.S.Ed from The University of Houston and a MDiv from Austin Presbyterian Theological Seminary.

Today, she pastors her local congregation as a "House of Prayer" with an emphasis on healing love and deep biblical discipleship. She is the founder and Executive Officer of HOST Ministries, which serves as a catalyst and tool in uniting people through Christ-based initiatives. She is involved in her local community and was awarded Cedar Park's "Citizen of the Year." Email: L77c@ aol.com

CAROLE LEWIS

After serving more than 30 years as National Director of First Place 4 Health, Carole Lewis now serves the organization as Director Emeritus. First Place 4 Health is an international Christ-centered health and wellness program. Carole has authored more than 40 books, including *Give God a Year: Change Your Life Forever* and *A Thankful Heart*. She is a warm, transparent, and humorous communicator and a sought-after speaker and conference leader and resides in the Houston, Texas area.

Dr. Kie Bowman

Dr. Kie Bowman is the author of numerous books including *I Am: A Biography of Jesus of Nazareth*. He is an active leader in the Southern Baptist Convention and has pastored growing churches in Texas and Georgia. Dr. Bowman preaches nationally and internationally and holds degrees in Ministry and Divinity. He is senior pastor of Hyde Park Baptist-The Quarries Church. He and his wife Tina have three adult children and make their home in Austin, Texas. www.hydeparkbaptistchurch.org

Rev. Brian Alarid

Brian Alarid was born in southern California and spent much of his childhood in Mexico, Costa Rica, and Guatemala, where his parents served as missionaries. While on the mission field, he became fluent in Spanish and developed a passion for missions.

Rev. Alarid is the founder and lead pastor of Passion Church in Albuquerque, New Mexico. He is a Regional Manager for the Billy Graham Evangelistic Association and Franklin Graham's Decision America Tour 2016. He is Co-Chairman of New Mexico Prays.

Brian has a Master's degree in Organizational Leadership from Regent University, and a Bachelor's degree in Theology. Brian has been married to Mercy Alarid for 19 years, and they reside in Albuquerque, New Mexico with their three children: Chloe, Colin and Lauren. Phone: 505-897-2232 Email: bdalarid@gmail.com Twitter: @BrianAlarid

Bible Versions & Translations

Scripture quotations marked (NIV) are taken from the Holy Bible, New International Version®, NIV®. Copyright© 1973, 1978, 1984, 2011 by Biblica, Inc.™ Used by permission of Zondervan. All rights reserved worldwide. <u>www.zondervan.com</u> The "NIV" and "New International Version" are trademarks registered in the United States Patent and Trademark Office by Biblica, Inc.™

Scripture quotations marked AMP are taken from the Amplified® Bible, Copyright © 1954, 1958, 1962, 1964, 1965, 1987 by The Lockman Foundation Used by permission." (<u>www.Lockman.org</u>)

Scripture quotations marked THE MESSAGE are taken from THE MESSAGE, copyright© by Eugene H. Person 1993, 1994, 1995, 1996, 2000, 2001, 2002. Used by permission of NavPress Publishing Group.

Scripture quotations marked HCSB are taken from the Holman Christian Standard Bible®, Copyright © 1999, 2000, 2002, 2003, 2009 by Holman Bible Publishers. Used by permission. Holman Christian Standard Bible®, Holman CSB®, and HCSB® are federally registered trademarks of Holman Bible Publishers.

Scripture quotations marked ICB are taken from the Holy Bible, International Children's Bible® Copyright© 1986, 1988, 1999, 2015 by Tommy Nelson™, a division of Thomas Nelson. Used by permission.

Scriptures marked NASU are taken from the NEW AMERICAN STANDARD UPDATED (NASU): Scripture taken from the NEW AMERICAN STANDARD UPDATED BIBLE®, copyright©, 1995 by The Lockman Foundation. Used by permission.

Scripture quotations marked NASB are taken from the New American Standard Bible®, Copyright © 1960, 1962, 1963, 1968, 1971, 1972, 1973, 1975, 1977, 1995 by The Lockman Foundation. Used by permission. (<u>www.Lockman.org</u>)

Scripture quotations market NLT are taken from the Holy Bible, New Living Translation, copyright ©1996, 2004, 2007 by Tyndale House Foundation. Used by permission of Tyndale House Publishers, Inc., Carol Stream, Illinois 60188. All rights reserved.

(ENDNOTES)

1   . Bradford, William, *Bradford's History of the Plymouth Settlement*, (1608-1650); as rendered into modern English by Harold Paget (E. P. Duggon: Colorado, 1920), p. 21; posted by Angie Mosteller, wwwcelebratingholidays.com

2   . Ibid.

3   . www.history.com/topics/pilgrims

4   . Hall and Holisher, p. 10; as referenced by Mendall Taylor, *Exploring Evangelism* (Kansas City, MO.: Beacon Hill Press, 1964), p. 361.

5   . *Reader's Digest*, September 2008, p. 86.

6   . Francis Canavan, S.J., in *Catholic Eye* (Nov. 18, 1987). *Christianity Today*, vol. 32, no. 3.

7   This article first appeared in Dr. Phil Ware's blog   https://onelife2love.wordpress.com/2009/07/27/persistence-in-prayer-will-bring-you-what-you-need/ Used by permission.

Made in the USA
Charleston, SC
08 March 2017